more
straight
TALK

Pastor Mark Jeske

Published by Straight Talk Books
P.O. Box 301, Milwaukee, WI 53201
800.661.3311 · timeofgrace.org

Cover image: Lightstock.com

Printed in the United States of America

ISBN: 978-1-942107-42-2

Contents

Introduction

Why?

Young children have been known to drive their parents and grandparents mad with their persistent questions. Why? Why?

"Why do cows have milk in their udders?" "Why do stars seem to twinkle?" "Why is the sky blue and the grass green?" "Why can't I watch that movie?" "Why do I have to go to bed?"

Sometimes their questions are spiritual in nature: "Why didn't God just kill the devil before he could tempt Adam and Eve?" "If Jesus can do anything, why didn't he make everybody a believer?"

And yet there is something far worse than an inquisitive child—a child (or grown-up) who has no curiosity at all. Questions show that the person is paying attention, cares, and is mentally engaged in the topic and *wants to know.* When Jesus was attending temple worship for the first time as an "adult," Luke's gospel tells us that his parents **"found him in the temple courts, sitting among the teachers, listening to them and** *asking them questions"* (2:46).

I hope you never lose your sense of childlike curiosity about who your God is, how he works, and how you fit into his agenda. Time of Grace is blessed with very inquisitive viewers and readers who are not shy about sending in their questions. I already answered a book full of their questions—*Straight Talk: Answers from God's Word.* So here in *More Straight Talk* are over 150 new head-scratchers that are answered to the degree that Scripture makes possible. We won't have all the answers till we get to heaven, where we shall know fully, even as we are fully known (1 Corinthians 13:12). But in the meantime, it's great fun to dig into the Word together.

Pastor Mark Jeske

1

"Your word, Lord, is eternal; it stands firm in the heavens"
(Psalm 119:89).

The Bible and Questions About God

Q: Is there any hard evidence of creation?

A: It is difficult even to have a conversation about creation and evolution between a Bible believer and unbeliever. If someone has decided in advance that the Bible is nonsense or a cute fairy tale with no basis in actual historical fact, none of the Bible's words will gain any traction.

What you can do in a discussion like that is to show that believing in evolution takes even more faith than creation. Here are some of the logical and scientific points creationists make:

- Even after centuries of assembling the "fossil record," there are still no transitional forms between species. The fossil record uniformly shows "stasis" (species stability). If evolution were true, you would expect to see many examples of one species turning into another.

- If you object to a sudden creation by an all-powerful deity, you then have to explain how matter and energy are eternal or else explain how something came from nothing. Both are huge leaps of faith.

- The second law of thermodynamics states that the universe is not gaining energy; rather, as time progresses *entropy* increases (i.e., chaos and loss of energy).

- Even science-based public TV shows like to use the word *designed* to describe the incredible complexity, beauty, and functionality in the animal world. To imagine that the inorganic world suddenly became organic, that plants became animals, and that animals became human *without any guidance* is unlikely to the point of absurdity. Even unbelievers have to take seriously the concept that there is intelligent design in our universe.

- Galaxies and space radiation are receding from us uniformly in every direction. That means that Earth, rather than being a tiny accidental blip in a corner of the massive universe, actually looks to be the center of everything.

You can find a wealth of creationist material on the websites of the Institute for Creation Research (Dallas, Texas) and Answers in Genesis/Creation Museum (Petersburg, Kentucky).

● ● ● ● ● ● ●

Q: Why did God create us in the first place?

A: It's not that the triune God was needy. God was serene and self-sufficient from all eternity. But God birthed the human race for many of the same reasons that husbands and wives long to become parents—to create miniature versions of themselves, with the same value system and philosophy of life, someone to love and from whom to receive love. Our

God is intensely relational, and he derives great satisfaction from receiving our worship, prayers, service, and gifts and in turn pouring out his blessings on us.

We were never created to be on our own. All things in creation, especially the people, but including even the holy angels, were woven together with Jesus Christ at the center: **"In him** (i.e., Christ) **all things were created: things in heaven and on earth, visible and invisible, whether thrones or powers or rulers or authorities; all things have been created through him and for him. He is before all things, and in him all things hold together"** (Colossians 1:16,17).

As God was forming a spiritual nation out of millions of former Egyptian slaves, he had Moses tell the Israelites at Mt. Sinai: **"If you obey me fully and keep my covenant, then out of all nations you will be my treasured possession. Although the whole earth is mine, you will be for me a kingdom of priests and a holy nation"** (Exodus 19:5,6).

You and I are not biological accidents. We are masterpieces of design and construction by the One who wants to know us and love us forever.

● ● ● ● ● ● ●

Q: Do the Old Testament rules still apply to us?

A: Some do. The trick is in knowing which.

The laws that God gave in Old Testament (i.e., pre-Christ) times are of three types. The first group includes *civil laws,* which applied to the people of Israel from the time of their becoming a nation until the coming of Christ. They are the laws of crime and punishment—simple, rough, and fast—designed for a time when the Israelites were a tribal society without police, court system, or jails. There were three simple levels of punishment for three levels of severity of offense: fines, corporal punishment, and capital punishment. It was never God's intent for these civil laws to be binding on all mankind in perpetuity.

The second type includes the *ceremonial laws*. God designed an elaborate framework for Israel's worship life in which he illustrated human brokenness and his wonderful master plan for restoration of that broken relationship. All of the great works of Jesus Christ for our salvation were acted out in advance, using animal substitutes for the great drama of condemnation, punishment, and forgiveness of sins. The animals that were slaughtered were temporary stand-ins for Christ, and the need for these sacrifices ended once and for all on Good Friday.

The ceremonial laws include also the regulations about kosher cooking. Those rules were intended to keep Israel separate, so that they would not be assimilated into the pagan societies surrounding them. There are no ceremonially "clean" and "unclean" foods for you and me today.

The laws that do apply to us, those that God had always intended to be timeless expressions of his holy will for all mankind of all times, are called the *moral law*. The way that we know they still apply to us today is that they have been repeated in the New Testament. Idolatry has been and still continues to be an offense to God, as is disrespect and disobedience to parents and those in authority, murder, adultery, theft, false witness, and coveting.

What the laws cannot do is save you. They can only shine a light on your brokenness. Jesus Christ kept all the laws for us (all three types), suffered the condemnation we deserved, and rose again to speak words of forgiveness. The moral laws now serve us as a guide to God-pleasing behaviors.

* * * * * * *

Q: Why don't we still see dramatic signs from God like the writing on the wall? Or is that just a fable?

A: That's actually two questions. First, the account isn't just a fable; it actually took place. If you read Daniel chapter 5, you can marvel at how God actually used his almighty power to create the illusion or presence of a large hand. The fingers of that giant hand held chalk or some other writing material and wrote four words on a wall of Emperor Belshazzar's royal palace in Babylon: MENE, MENE, TEKEL, PARSIN.

The words were a riddle that Daniel was able to interpret: Belshazzar's days as emperor had been numbered; he had been weighed and found wanting; his kingdom would be given to the Medes and Persians. That night in 539 B.C. the Lord actually delivered the Babylonian empire into the hands of Cyrus the Persian and Darius the Mede.

But the other part of the question is maybe a little more urgent: why don't we still see dramatic signs from God like that? Well, realize that in ancient times the full Bible had not yet been written. God chose to do more direct communications with people because not as much of the "signpost" of his written Word was available to people.

But I'm not so sure that we don't still see signs of God's direct working today. God still is intervening in our human history and intervening in our lives, making things happen. The fact that people don't notice God at work doesn't mean he isn't at work. He is still the Lord of history; he still causes nations to rise up and will bring the evil ones crashing down. With guidance from the Bible, you and I can get a sense of

God's wonderful agenda to draw us closer to him.

And be careful of what you wish for! There were a lot of people at Jesus' time who *saw* all his miraculous signs. It was a very sign-rich time to be living in the land of Israel. And though people saw his signs, they missed all the *meaning* and in fact viewed Jesus as an enemy. If you want to see signs of what God is going to do, pay attention to your Bible, pay attention to your world, and watch God keep his promises.

● ● ● ● ● ● ●

Q: Are dinosaurs mentioned in the Bible?

A: The short answer is no. They are never mentioned by name.

God would have created them along with everything else during creation week, of course. It is part of the rhythm of God's world, however, that species have been going extinct for millennia. Perhaps the dinosaurs' time was over even before the great flood (Genesis 6–9). If any were loaded onto Noah's ark, they might have been young (and of course small) examples of the species. If any came off the ark, they must not have lasted long. Perhaps there were climate changes on Earth after the great flood that hastened their extinction. They did not play into any of the biblical narratives.

The Bible does make reference to large land and sea animals that cannot be identified with any particular species. The Hebrew word *tannin* could describe a crocodile, sea monster, or dragon. The New Testament Greek word *drakon* (dragon) refers, of course, to a beast that is mythological; it is a horrifying descriptor of the devil in Revelation chapter 12. Dragons never existed, but it just may be that there were some old human memories that were passed down in oral tradition of a huge beast with a long scaly tail and ferociously sharp teeth.

* * * * * * *

Q: I just read 1 Samuel chapter 28. Why did God allow a medium to bring up Samuel, a child of God, to talk to Saul if God tells us to steer clear of supernatural things like mediums and psychics?

A: God did indeed tell his Old Testament believers, and you and me, to stay away from any kinds of sorcery, black magic, the occult, or Satanism, and that includes séances or any effort to resurrect or communicate with the dead. **"When someone tells you to consult mediums and spiritists, who whisper and mutter, should not a people inquire of their God? Why consult the dead on behalf of the living? Consult God's instruction and the testimony of warning. If anyone does not speak according to this word, they have no light of dawn"** (Isaiah 8:19,20). As Jesus taught in his parable of the rich man and Lazarus, there is a great gulf fixed between the blessed saints in heaven and the lives of those still on the earth.

So how did the events of 1 Samuel chapter 28 happen? One possibility is that Satan created an illusion of Samuel through a medium, who had been dabbling in the occult before. Satan's goal would have been to torment or deceive Saul even further than he was already, as well as offer alternatives to the Word of God as sources of spiritual authority and power.

I think it more likely that the spirit of Samuel was authentic, that he was sent by God as a public judgment on

Saul because of his unbelief and disobedience. God can make his own exceptions to the rules he lays on us. I think God decided that words of condemnation coming from Samuel one last time would be a powerful finale to the life of a king who had shown so much promise but who fell so far. Spirit-Samuel's voice in 1 Samuel chapter 28 sounds very similar to the words he spoke while alive to Saul in 1 Samuel 15:28-35.

Everything he said was correct, and everything he predicted came true (not the usual modus operandi of Satan the liar). Note finally that spirit-Samuel spoke *directly* to Saul, not through the medium or in any way under her control.

* * * * * * *

Q: How can we be sure that the biblical accounts of Jesus' death are accurate? Did he really rise from the dead?

A: Really two questions here. The first is on the reliability of the historical information in Scripture. The Bible makes the powerful claim that all its content came straight from God, that the prophets and apostles were only God's human instruments for the Holy Spirit's information (2 Peter 1:21). That means that whatever is described as a historical occurrence really did happen.

Realize that Satan's only chance to peel you away from God's family and lure you into his death trap is to lead you to doubt the Word of God. The Word has its own power to persuade, its own power to create faith in its life-giving message. Just read it and the certainty will grow. Don't talk *about* the resurrection, read Scripture's account directly. Read them all—each of the four gospels has a unique slant on Easter.

The second question is whether the Scripture actually

teaches a resurrection of the physical body of Christ. It does indeed. Jesus was truly dead. Respiration and pulse had ceased. An EKG performed on him as he was lowered from the cross would have shown a flatline. But early on Easter morning, his physical body actually came back to life. Brain activity, heartbeat, and breathing began again. His cold skin became warm. He moved on his own and walked out of his cave tomb. His mouth spoke once again. He was touched by his disciples and ate fish with them.

Jesus' physical resurrection is a big deal because it guarantees God's love for you, guarantees the forgiveness of your sins, and guarantees *your* resurrection on the Last Day.

● ● ● ● ● ● ●

Q: Pastor Jeske, after Jesus, who is your all-time favorite person mentioned in the Bible and why?

A: Ah, so many heroes, so many role models, so many sources of inspiration in Scripture. If I had to pick just one, I guess it would be Daniel.

Daniel was taken from his home in Judah as a teenager, and he never saw his home again. He spent his entire life in Babylon, working in government service for the nation that had destroyed his. His boss, Nebuchadnezzar, had led the assault that resulted in the complete destruction of Jerusalem and its beautiful temple.

And yet Daniel's work *in Babylon* was extremely useful to God, whose agenda involved having his man promoted repeatedly until he was essentially chancellor of the entire province of Babylon.

I find it inspirational that Daniel's life and dreams seemed to be yanked away from him. He trudged hundreds of miles with the rest of the captives, thinking that his life was ruined. Perhaps he feared that the Israelite nation and its special identity and mission were ruined too. But over time he saw that both his life and his nation were still in God's hands and plans. He became a voice for the God of Israel in that strange land, speaking God's blessings and God's judgments on the mighty. Daniel lived long enough to see the fall of mighty Babylon and hear the proclamation of Cyrus the Persian that the Jews could return home.

Daniel's story is an encouragement to all of us whose lives seem to be derailed by unforeseen events, encouragement to go with the flow and see how God can use us in ways different from what we had imagined. Daniel's life helps me not obsess so much about being in control and helps me pay attention to how God would like to use me each day.

• • • • • • •

Q: Why are there so many metaphors in the Bible? Some of them are so confusing!

A: They are indeed. Jesus' own disciples struggled to understand and interpret his parables. Picture language is deliberately a little ambiguous—the point of using figures of speech is to highlight emotion and intensity. Precision is for prose.

You might not understand the figurative language at first read. Join the crowd—I didn't either. Just keep reading and studying your Bible. Take notes when you figure something out, or when a passage in a different place clarifies the puzzle for you. Mastery of the Bible's many styles comes with experience—each year that you stay at it you will grow in your grasp of the main message.

Jesus didn't invent figures of speech for his teaching—he was following a long tradition of Old Testament spokesmen for God who used dramatic language full of metaphors, similes, hyperbole, double entendres, contrasts, parables, assonance, rhythmic meter, flashbacks, foreshadowing, and every other literary device you can think of, all to make their message memorable.

Just think how precious some of the metaphors for the Savior himself have become to our worship and prayer life—Christ the Lamb of God, Christ the Lion of the tribe of Judah, Christ the Good Shepherd, Christ the Vine, and Christ the heavenly Bridegroom.

And for those figures of speech that you still struggle to understand, that's why commentaries, Bible dictionaries, and online resources exist.

● ● ● ● ● ● ●

Q: Why is the Trinity necessary? If God is all-powerful, why did he need to send Jesus and the Holy Spirit?

A: First of all, it's not a matter of the Trinity's being necessary or not. The Bible just gives us God's self-revelation. This is who he is—one in three and three in one. God acts and speaks sometimes as one God and sometimes acts and speaks in three persons—Father, Son, and Spirit. It is an unsolvable divine mystery; Scripture tells us about him not so that we *understand* but so that we *believe*.

The triune God was present at creation. The Spirit brooded over the muddy mess before God's six creative words were spoken. When it came time for the creation of humanity, God said, **"Let *us* make mankind in our image"**

(Genesis 1:26). The prologue to St. John's gospel tells us that Jesus Christ, the Son, had his divine "fingers" in all aspects of creation—**"without him nothing was made that has been made"** (1:3).

From all eternity God planned the creation of the physical universe and the creation of dear people he intended to be his multitude of children. From all eternity he knew that his first children would betray him and choose evil, and from all eternity the triune God resolved on a plan that would send the Son to Earth to take on human flesh. In this way he would relive our lives for us and die our death for us.

From all eternity the triune God resolved that it should be the Spirit's great work to bring faith to the hearts of lost people, bring spiritual gifts for them to use, and bind the believers together in unity. Did the Father *need* to send Jesus and the Spirit? I don't know if there could have been any other way to bring you and me back to God, and I'm mighty glad for the work of the Father, Son, and Spirit on my behalf.

● ● ● ● ● ● ●

Q: Do the Holy Spirit, Jesus, and God the Father have different jobs? Or do they all do the same thing?

A: Both statements are true—yet another of Scripture's paradoxes. The Bible tells us that the three persons of the Trinity have different roles—only the Son took on human flesh, suffered, and died; only the Spirit proceeds from the Father and the Son. It is the Spirit who inspired the writing of the Holy Scriptures and who uses that Word to bring people to faith and keep them in faith.

But there is also an essential unity of purpose within the Trinity. The Bible usually speaks of God in the singular, and when it does, referring to "God" or "The LORD," you may assume that the three persons are speaking and working together in concert. Father, Son, and Holy Spirit together willed the universe into existence at the time of creation; Father, Son, and Holy Spirit together desire the salvation of all people.

● ● ● ● ● ● ●

Q: Is it bad to refer to God as "him" because he isn't a human? How do we know God is a man?

A: First of all, remember that the second person of the Trinity, Jesus Christ, the Son of God from all eternity, *is* actually human. He took on human flesh and fused it with his divine existence, and the human being that he became was a biological male. It is proper always to use masculine pronouns when referring to Jesus Christ.

Second, even before the Son became incarnate, Scripture in the Old Testament exclusively uses masculine pronouns to refer to God. The New Testament does as well. The eternal God is not a man, but the Bible always uses male terminology. The relationship between the first two persons is always described as Father/Son, never Mother/Daughter. God is spirit, but that doesn't mean that the wondrous subject of gender is not involved somehow. The first woman, Eve, is said to have been made in the image of God as well as Adam.

The divine nature of God is a mystery that we will never penetrate fully and need to respect. All we have to go on is the language of Scripture, and so we will limit ourselves to that, praising *his* holy name.

The fuller revelation in heaven will come soon.

· · · · · · ·

Q: Does God sleep or get tired?

A: God is awake and alert and on duty 24/7. Psalm 121:3,4 tells us, **"He who watches over you will not slumber; indeed, he who watches over Israel will neither slumber nor sleep."** Isn't that an amazing statement both of comfort and awe? God never rests. He sustains the universe constantly and never grows old or runs out of energy. He intently watches your life and never loses interest. He is constantly making decisions on what to allow, what to stop, and how and when to intervene in your life. Satan can never sneak anything past God because one who never sleeps can't be caught napping.

Interestingly enough, when Jesus took on human flesh, he had to learn to care for his human body just like us. He needed breaks for emotional and physical rest, and he most certainly needed to sleep each night just as we do. In fact his sleeping once terrified the disciples. Jesus was so exhausted that he fell asleep in their boat on the Sea of Galilee and slept through a terrific storm. **"The disciples went and woke him, saying, 'Lord, save us! We're going to drown!'"** (Matthew 8:25).

That wonderful example of Jesus' humanity encourages us to trust that he doesn't despise us for our weaknesses because he too experienced physical weakness. The spirit indeed is willing, but our flesh is weak. When you pray to Jesus for strength, his heart is inclined to help you because he remembers what exhaustion feels like.

· · · · · · ·

Q: How did God exist when there was nothing? Where did he come from?

A: As always, the only reliable place to go for information about God is his Word. Philosophical speculation or scientific inquiry won't help us. The Bible tells us that God is eternal. He is endless in both directions—forward and backward. He is the one who is and who was and who is to come. He was not created. He has no origin or beginning—he just always existed and always will. He didn't come *from* anywhere—his power, mind, perception, will, and spirit fill the entire universe. Is that a mystery? Sure is.

The Trinity existed from all eternity, serene and all-sufficient, Father, Son, and Spirit coexisting and timeless. The reason why *we* exist is that the Lord desired to love and be loved, to create miniature versions of himself who would have his value system. We were made to speak and act in accordance with God's goodness and to return God's great love for us with love for him and for each other.

● ● ● ● ● ● ●

Q: My teenagers are starting to question as to whether God really exists. We're experiencing some really tough things in our family, and I can see why they doubt. I just don't know how to convince them. Can you help?

A: First of all, I like your attitude that you're not going to shame them or bully them or pressure them or mock them for having doubts. I like that you take them seriously. Teens are furious when their parents treat them like little children. You build a foundation of trust when you acknowledge that there might be some rationale behind what they say. You allow them to speak without fear, even when they say things that aren't politically correct in a Christian family. You don't rush to smack down something that sounds dumb to you. In this way you show that you are not afraid of a challenge, because God's Word is tough enough and true enough to stand on its own.

Second, you can then lead them into Scripture to show where other people have been wounded or hurt or wondered, "Where is God?" Let them read the prophet Habakkuk, for instance, and his aching questions that he has for God. But then take them to Hebrews chapter 12 and allow them to see that a loving God sometimes blesses us with spoiling us with treats and treasures and sometimes he blesses us with hardships. Character is not developed through pampering. Character and strength of our own personal faith only grow and develop when we're stressed.

Third, you can help your kids work through tough times by reminding them of the multitude of blessings and rescues that your family has experienced in the past. You can recall how God sent friends and helpers into your life at just the right time, and he will do that again. Show them that you're not afraid; model for them how strong people show patience.

Above all, let God's Word speak to their doubts and their needs. You don't have to put all the pressure on yourself to overpower their wrong ideas because of your own wonderful persuasion or debate skills or how logical you can be or how powerful you can sound. Just let God talk, and then trust that the Word will do its work. Let them hear Scripture's promises that **"in all things God works for the good of those who love him, who have been called according to his purpose"** (Romans 8:28).

And when he does deliver you, remember to thank him with your family.

• • • • • • •

Q: Why do you think it was necessary for Mary and Joseph to have such a tough time when Jesus came as a baby? Why did he need to be born under such dangerous conditions with Herod at their heels and in a barn of all places?

A: The Bible never tells us that all of the strange events surrounding the birth of Christ were *necessary*. It just tells us that they happened.

It wasn't all bad. There were plenty of blessings: The birth was safe and successful. Joseph did not have to deal with a breech delivery. Mary (apparently) did not suffer any childbirth traumas. As soon as he could, Joseph got her into a house (where they were living when the Magi came to visit). The scriptural prophecy from Micah chapter 5 about the place of the Savior's birth in little Bethlehem was fulfilled. They made it.

But there were hardships too. Even though people in those days were much closer to the nitty-gritty of birth and death, still Joseph must have been stressed to the max to deliver his first child in the dark in an animal pen. But such is the way of life of the poor of all centuries—they suffer many indignities and shortcomings. It was part of Jesus' humble service as our Savior that from the very beginning he experienced hardship and deprivation. He became poor indeed to make us rich.

He also experienced the direct attacks of Satan. The enraged lord of hell was in full attack mode, knowing that he had a willing helper in Herod. The assassination attempt (Matthew 2) was so massive that it nearly succeeded, but though other babies were slaughtered, an angelic dream messenger tipped off the holy family so that they fled the country. There would be many more satanic attacks, but Jesus triumphed over them all.

* * * * * * *

Q: Jesus came to the world to save us from our sins. But why did he come as a baby? Couldn't God have sent him as an adult and sped up the process?

A: It was always God's plan to send the Messiah as an actual human descendant of Mother Eve. In Genesis 3:15, God told his fallen daughter that her *Offspring* would crush the head of Satan, the serpent. Seven centuries before Christmas Eve, the prophet Isaiah revealed to Israel, **"To us a child is born; to us a son is given"** (Isaiah 9:6).

Why should that be necessary? First of all, it is essential to God's plan for our salvation that Jesus would reenact the entire human experience, including being an unborn child in Mary's womb from the moment of conception. He really came to be every man and every woman, to relive our lives for us, and that means he had to do everything right that we had done wrong, going all the way back to childhood. You need the experience of childhood dependence on your parents; you need the experience of how to obey your parents in spite of your teenage impulses to lash out, to strike out on your own and rebel.

For another, God didn't need to speed up the process. He had been waiting for over four millennia already, and he was not in a hurry. In fact, Jesus' public ministry was very short, wasn't it? Maybe three years. And so it wasn't the *quantity* of time that God was interested in but the *quality* of the experience that led Jesus Christ to become fully human. In this way he could bring his precious forgiveness to every man, woman, and child who's ever lived because he is our perfect Substitute.

• • • • • • •

Q: Why did Jesus have to actually die for our sins? Couldn't God have found another way that Jesus could remain living and stay on earth forever? It would be so much more believable if he was still here.

A: Jesus himself racked his brains for other ways to win back the people of the world. As he prayed in torment of soul in the Garden of Gethsemane, **"'Father,' he said, 'everything is possible for you. Take this cup from me. Yet not what I will, but what you will'"** (Mark 14:36). The Father's answer: there is no other way.

God's central dilemma is this: how can I both punish sinners and forgive sinners? For thousands of years he had been telling people that there would be fearful judgment coming down upon all unbelievers and evildoers. But at the same time he was promising grace and mercy to hopeless and helpless people. The only way in which these two commitments of God could both be kept was through a Substitute.

As a human being Jesus could come to earth and offer his perfect obedience in place of our terrible disobedience. He was the ultimate Substitute, and because he was also true God, his perfect life could be applied to all people. On Calvary the Father had it both ways—both of his pronouncements were true. He both punished the sins of the world by punishing Jesus, and he could show mercy because he could now see the world through "Jesus-tinted glasses."

Jesus wanted his disciples to see that his ascension

into heaven was not abandonment. They would have much preferred to have him resume his traveling teaching ministry. But he had powerful reasons for ascending to heaven: 1) His return to heaven was his coronation; 2) His ascension ushered in the massive outpouring of the Holy Spirit; 3) His ascension was a huge promotion for the disciples (and us). *We* are now the proclaimers of the Word.

Jesus is still present in spirit. He watches over us, directs the holy angels on our behalf, and is close enough to hear our prayers in his name. His voice still comes to us through the gospels, and he still feeds us with the heavenly food of himself in the Lord's Supper. Soon, soon we will see him again. In the flesh!

● ● ● ● ● ● ●

Q: Did Jesus and the disciples drink wine? Or were they not allowed to "enjoy life" like that?

A: God is the inventor of wine and the grapes that make it possible. He intended it to be a gift to us—it **"gladdens human hearts"** (Psalm 104:15). Paul recommended to Timothy that he drink a little more wine to improve his digestion (1 Timothy 5:23). While abuse of alcohol is a terrible feature of human life, it is not the fault of the wine. Individual Christians may choose not to drink, but they should not impose their personal decisions on others as moral commandments.

Jesus and his disciples most certainly drank wine. Vineyards were a basic fruit crop in ancient Israel, and wine was how the precious juice of the grape could be preserved in an age before mechanical refrigeration. Wine and water were the two basic table beverages. It was a critical part of every

Passover meal, and Jesus chose it to be part of the Lord's Supper that he instituted.

Take a few minutes to read John chapter 2. It is important to ponder Jesus' very first miracle, the very first time that he chose to break the ordinary laws of nature and do something important to advance the kingdom and build faith in people. He and his disciples were attending a wedding whose reception suffered an embarrassing shortage of wine. Did the event have unexpected extra guests or just poor planning? The Bible doesn't say.

What it does say is that Jesus chose that moment to rescue the bride and groom and their bridal reception. He instructed the servers to fill six large water jars, and he turned the water into wine. So to answer your question, yes, Jesus and his disciples enjoyed wine, and Jesus created 120 gallons of it to help a lot of other people enjoy it too.

* * * * * * *

Q: Do we know anything about how long Jesus was in hell when he descended? And how long was Jesus actually in his grave? The Bible says that Jesus predicted, "After three days, I will rise again," but it seems to me if people count hours, it's far less a time than three full days; far fewer than 72 hours. So what is the chronology here?

A: The four gospels don't spell out the sequence of events and specify the days by name. So we need to assemble the chronology from various pieces. First, there can be no doubt that the holy resurrection took place early on Sunday morning. **"Early on the *first day of the week*, while it was still dark, Mary Magdalene went to the tomb and saw that the stone had been removed from the entrance"** (John 20:1).

The day of Pilate's fateful "trial" and death sentence for Jesus was **"the day of Preparation, and the next day was to be a special Sabbath"** (John 19:31). In Old Testament times, the Sabbath was the seventh day (i.e., Saturday). So the day before it, the Day of Preparation, would have been Friday, and thus most of Christendom observes the death of Christ on the Friday we call "Good." Nicodemus and Joseph removed the body from the cross, gave it a quick wrapping with linen and spices, and interred it in Joseph's cave. They had to hustle to be done working by 6:00 P.M. when the official Jewish Saturday Sabbath began.

Thus Jesus would have been in the tomb late Friday afternoon through Sunday morning—*parts* of three days but clearly not three *full* days. Jesus' own reference to the similarity of his and Jonah's three-day "burial" (Matthew 12:40) would thus be understood as an interesting parallel, not a literal accounting of minutes spent in the grave.

The Bible tells us that though dead in the body, *in spirit* Jesus descended to the pit of hell to proclaim his victory to Satan and the souls of the unbelieving and disobedient rebels imprisoned there (see 1 Peter 3:19,20). There is no mention of the duration of time of that visit. It didn't need to be long—it wasn't a teaching tour, for those in hell will never again have the chance to repent. It was his victory lap after all Satan had put him through. It was the champion standing over the crushed head of the serpent. His wonderful spirit then returned to the cave and rejoined his body, bringing it back to life.

● ● ● ● ● ● ●

Q: Did Jesus really never sin?

A: Correct. The Bible leaves no doubt: **"Since we have a great high priest who has ascended into heaven, Jesus the Son of God, let us hold firmly to the faith we profess. For we do not have a high priest who is unable to empathize with our weaknesses, but we have one who has been tempted in every way, just as we are—*yet he did not sin*"** (Hebrews 4:14,15).

This is a big deal. If Jesus had failed even once, in thought, word, or deed, all would have been lost. He himself would have fallen under God's judgment just like us, and there would have been no one to save us.

But he did it. He actually lived his entire 33 years successfully fighting off Satan's temptations, severe as they were. He obeyed every law of Caesar, Israel, and God. The best part? His perfection is attributed to us through our faith in him. God now looks on us and considers us to be as sinless as his perfect Son. How can we not be crazy in love with him and strive to honor him and live up to that magnificent gift?

● ● ● ● ● ● ●

Q: How is it that so many religions came about with such differing views of who Jesus Christ is?

A: The short answer is Satan. Satan has a terrific interest in keeping people confused and distant from Jesus, because the Savior is his worst nightmare. Only Jesus threatens his hold on people; only faith in Jesus can pry us loose and set us on the path to heaven. The devil works overtime to lure people into believing false information. This keeps their minds open to the substitute messiahs he wishes to provide.

Only the Bible has clear and accurate information about the person and work of our Savior Jesus. That's where Satan launches his attacks—anything to distract and confuse and mislead people from the true Word. Sometimes he is able to persuade Christians that large sections of the Bible are of human origin, not from God, and thus can be accepted or rejected as one pleases. Actually that attitude is kind of exciting—instead of submitting yourself humbly to the Bible, you set yourself *over* the Bible and pass judgment as you see fit over what is true and what is disposable.

Some religions are only partly based on Scripture, and they have other sacred books that in fact trump the Bible's authority and information. Others don't bother with the Bible at all, though they may give Jesus a nod for the bits and pieces of his ministry that they find useful to their philosophy.

Pay no attention to those distractions. The apostle John tells us that all of the accounts in his gospel were written **"that you may believe that Jesus is the Messiah, the Son of God, and that by believing you may have life in his name"** (John 20:31). You can trust the Bible's information, authority, and power because it comes to you straight from God himself.

●　●　●　●　●　●　●

Q: What does the Holy Spirit do?

A: The Spirit has been active ever since creation, ever since he brooded over the watery chaos before the ordered creation began. He works in concert with the Father and Son for all the things they do jointly.

First, it is the Spirit's special work to take the redemption that Christ Jesus bought for the world and connect it to people personally. He does that by "in*spir*ing" the writing of the Holy Scriptures. **"Prophets, though human, spoke from God as they were carried along by the Holy Spirit"** (2 Peter 1:21). Old Testament too—King David was very conscious of being the vehicle for writing down God's own words: **"The Spirit of the LORD spoke through me; his word was on my tongue"** (2 Samuel 23:2).

Second, the Spirit alone brings the power to convert people from unbelief to faith. The gospel in the Word is the power of salvation. **"No one can say, 'Jesus is Lord,' except by the Holy Spirit"** (1 Corinthians 12:3). You can't self-synthesize your own faith. It must be given to you. The Spirit works through the Word, but also through Word + water, i.e., Baptism: **"He saved us through the washing of rebirth and renewal by the Holy Spirit"** (Titus 3:5).

Third, it is the great work of the Spirit to give special gifts to each believer: **"Now to each one the manifestation of the Spirit is given for the common good. There are different kinds of gifts, but the same Spirit distributes them"** (1 Corinthians 12:7,4).

Finally, I might mention that the Spirit is your personal prayer courier, editor, and wingman. **"The Spirit helps us in our weakness. We do not know what we ought to pray for, but the Spirit himself intercedes for us through wordless groans. And he who searches our hearts knows the mind of the Spirit, because the Spirit intercedes for God's people in accordance with the will of God"** (Romans 8:26,27).

• • • • • • • •

Q: Is the Holy Spirit as important as the Father and Jesus? He doesn't seem to come up a lot in the Bible.

A: *Au contraire, mon ami!* The Scripture is loaded with references to the Holy Spirit, our Friend, Advocate, Counselor, Coach, Intermediary, Power Source, Truth-Revealer, and Gift-Giver. Watch for references to the Spirit's person and work as you read your Bible devotionally. Tag the references with a yellow highlighter, and they will jump off the page.

That includes the Old Testament. Sometimes people think that the Spirit began his work only on the Day of Pentecost. Not true. Just check a concordance, if you don't believe me, and look up how often the phrase "The Spirit of the Lord" occurs in the Old Testament. What changed on Pentecost was that God absolutely *poured* out Spirit-power and Spirit-gifts on that day and thereafter.

The Spirit is co-equal with the Father and the Son and is worthy of equal honor, praise, prayers, and adoration. What you might have been noticing is that Christians, and the Christian church, give so much emphasis to the work of Christ that the Spirit's mighty works seem underappreciated. That's unfortunate but sort of understandable. It is easy to visualize Jesus—Christendom is full of works of art portraying him in various scenes from his ministry. It's harder to illustrate the Spirit. All we have to work with is the image of a dove and flames of fire.

Urge your pastor to set aside a series of Sundays each year to dig into Scripture's treasury of teaching and bring out its wealth of Spirit-teaching. Dig in yourself, and let the Spirit help you discover the important spiritual gifts that he has placed within you.

● ● ● ● ● ● ●

Q: I've heard of the "sin against the Holy Spirit." What is that?

A: The passage to which you refer is from Luke 12:10: **"Everyone who speaks a word against the Son of Man will be forgiven."** That is a statement of purest gospel hope. It calls to mind the first words to come from Jesus' mouth on the cross, words of mercy toward the people who were tormenting him: "Father, forgive them." Jesus extended love and hope to Judas the betrayer and Peter the denier, even to his Roman crucifiers.

Jesus followed that statement of mercy with a stern statement of judgment: **"But anyone who blasphemes against the Holy Spirit will not be forgiven."** When people willfully and persistently reject the gospel, ignore and mock the Word of God that the Spirit has provided, they cut themselves off from the very power source they need to believe the gospel and be saved. They cut their own lifeline.

It is a somber and dreadful thought that some people are hardened in their condemnation while they are still alive and on this earth. For some, judgment day comes early. This is an earnest warning from Jesus to seize the moment. Now is the time to recognize and acknowledge your sins. Now is the time to repent. Now is the time to turn to your Savior Jesus. Now is the time to believe his wonderful promises of forgiveness and life. Now is the time to let the Spirit speak his words to straighten out your attitude and life.

* * * * * * *

Q: What does it mean to "walk in the Spirit"?

A: I think the verse you are referring to is Galatians 5:16:

"Walk by the Spirit, and you will not gratify the desires of the flesh." St. Paul in all his letters writes urgently about the need for believers to live their faith and show that their churchy talk translates into authentic day-to-day discipleship. It's all about what drives you.

When you are motivated and driven by your sinful appetites, only bad things come out. Paul has a lengthy paragraph in Galatians chapter 5 listing the damaging behaviors of people who follow "the flesh," things like sexual immorality, hatred, envy, and drunkenness. **"Those who live like this will not inherit the kingdom of God"** (verse 21). Instead, Christians, if you truly are grafted onto Jesus, the true Vine, you will be living branches and will bear fruit. Among them he lists love, kindness, gentleness, and self-control. **"Since we live by the Spirit, let us keep in step with the Spirit"** (verse 25).

A life of love and service is not optional for believers. It is the absolutely inevitable result of true faith. Let it flow in your life! Let the Spirit into your heart through his wonderful Word. Let the Spirit shape your value system, what you admire and pursue, and how you spend your money and your time.

Walk your talk.

2

*"Praise be to the God and Father of our Lord Jesus Christ . . .
who comforts us in all our troubles, so that we can
comfort those in any trouble with the comfort we
ourselves receive from God"* (2 Corinthians 1:3,4).

The Church

Q: What is turning people off from organized Christian
religion?

A: Jesus himself cautioned his disciples against thinking
that their ministries would bring about a Golden Age in
world history in which eventually everyone would become
a believer. He predicted, correctly, that over time Satan's
strength would grow and that **"the love of most will grow
cold"** (Matthew 24:12).

Things will ultimately get so bad that Satan will get
overconfident enough to muster his forces and attempt a
final battle to wipe the church from the face of the earth. The
Lord, however, will not let that happen, and that's when the
end will come. In other words, people will grow more self-
centered and turn against not only "organized" religion but
disorganized religion too. They will not want to submit to *any*
spiritual authority of *any* kind.

The most rapidly growing segment of the North
American population (catching up with Europe) is the group
of agnostics, atheists, and "nothings." Close to that group

are the "spiritual but not religious" people who assemble a mishmash of bits and pieces of religious ideas and practices that appeal to them. They like the feeling of being in control of their personal philosophy.

Why are these things happening?

- The wealthier and more powerful people get, the less they think we need God.

- Belief in evolution. If people think God did not design and build the world, then we aren't accountable to him or anybody.

- Media celebrities, our royalty, pander to human appetites and glorify freedom from restraint.

- People today reject absolute truth; "truth" today is only "my truth" and "your truth."

- People today reject authority of any kind—"Nobody tells me what to believe."

It's not all the fault of the people. I think also that "organized Christian religion" has often turned people off:

- When the church's message is based on politics and pop psychology instead of the simple power and changeless truth of God's Word.

- When Christian communities are full of cliques and hidebound traditionalism instead of warmth and genuine affection.

- When church leadership spends its energy pampering the increasingly shrinking membership instead of connecting with unchurched people in the community.

- When older leaders cling to their positions and are slow

to allow younger people to lead and bring in new ideas.

- When the only thing people see is arguing, criticizing, church politics, or fighting.

On the other hand, I think there is a genuine (and possibly quiet) spiritual revival going on all the time—just sometimes in a way church people are not noticing. The digital communication revolution spreads online trash all over the world, but it is spreading the gospel of Jesus as well to every corner of the globe. Although many local congregations are shrinking and closing, there are some insanely successful mega churches that have found how to draw people into the Word.

As Jesus urges us, let's work while it is day, not allowing hardships and obstacles to give us excuses to grind to a halt and stay silent about the best news in the world.

* * * * * * *

Q: How do we know that Christianity is actually the correct religion?

A: First off, let me state my opinion that Christianity is not a religion. I like to call it *reality*. When people hear the word *religion*, they think of it as a set of personal preferences, like which types of cuisine you prefer or whether you work out with yoga, weights, Pilates, running, or martial arts.

Christianity alone offers a comprehensive explanation for the origin of the universe, the origin of and purpose for mankind, and definitive answers to what comes after death. Christianity alone connects people with the very power of heaven to believe and live in accordance with God's plans and will. The Bible is the only reliable source of information on the true nature of God and the amazing things he has done in human history.

The ability to believe the preceding paragraph comes from God himself, who uses the message of the Bible to convince us of its truth. It's a treasure trove of information that is available nowhere else. St. Paul calls the Christian gospel the "power of God for salvation." Jesus told his disciples a few hours before his crucifixion that he alone was the Way, the Truth, and the Life. No one can have a real relationship with the Father in heaven except through him.

I don't like to think of the Christian faith as just one of many legitimate life philosophies. Like gravity, electromagnetism, and molecular attraction, it is simply reality.

* * * * * * * *

Q: Why do some church bodies allow for women pastors and some don't?

A: The worship life for most of the history of God's people has been led by men, as God designed. In the 15 centuries of Old Covenant worship before the time of Christ, the priests were required to be males only—Aaron and his sons and their male descendants. The Lord Jesus was not merely some sort of nonsexual or generic human being but was born a biological male, and he chose 12 males as his disciples and apostles. In the 19 centuries after Christ, pastors and priests were male. It was only in the beginning of the 20th century that some Pentecostal groups began ordaining women, and a half-century later some of the more liberal Protestant groups began to do it as well. The Roman Catholic Church has an all-male priesthood, and the more conservative and

evangelical wing of Christianity has only male pastors
as well.

The liberal Protestant denominations do not accept the
doctrine of the inerrancy and divine authorship of every
word of Scripture. They believe that all the books of the
Bible are of human origin and authorship and thus their
teachings can be changed with the times. Their decision to
ordain women was driven not so much by biblical study as by
changes in modern society and the feminist movement.

For those who still base their teachings on an inerrant
Scripture, the decisive verses are 1 Timothy 2:11,12: **"A
woman should learn in quietness and full submission. I do
not permit a woman to teach or to assume authority over
a man; she must be quiet."** This does not mean that women
have nothing to say. Every believing daughter of God is a
royal priest with a priestly personal ministry. On the day of
Pentecost, St. Peter quoted the prophet Joel that "your sons
and daughters will prophesy." The key word from 1 Timothy
chapter 2 is *authority*. In a congregation the pastor has the
last word on interpretation of Scripture, and that role God
has reserved for his men.

● ● ● ● ● ● ●

Q: If nothing can separate us from the love of Christ
(Romans 8:38,39), how can a believer reject Christ and
therefore be condemned?

A: These are two separate concepts and should not be
smooshed together. This is one of the many paradoxes of
Scripture, and we need to allow the two seemingly conflicting
ideas to stand on their own and not try to force them into the
logic of our own rational system.

The gospel of the love of Jesus Christ is *unconditional.* The sins of the *whole world* were atoned for by Christ (1 John 2:2). His love and saving work were not just for some, but were graciously given to all. No condemned person in hell can shout at God that he was selective in his grace. *All* were justified freely (Romans 3:24).

But the twin concept of grace is faith. We are saved by grace through faith. God's grace is upon all, but only some believe. We must not try to rationalize that seeming contradiction but just let it be. The hard truth is that some people will never believe the gospel, and even worse, some who believed it for a time grow weary of it and throw it away. Scripture shows us that this can happen and gives us a grave warning lest it happen to us: **"It is impossible for those who have once been enlightened, who have tasted the heavenly gift, who have shared in the Holy Spirit, who have tasted the goodness of the word of God and the powers of the coming age and who have fallen away, to be brought back to repentance. To their loss they are crucifying the Son of God all over again and subjecting him to public disgrace"** (Hebrews 6:4-6).

So should we rest serenely in the arms of Jesus or should we be vigilant against the devil's whispers and temptations to commit spiritual suicide? Yes.

● ● ● ● ● ● ●

Q: Pastor Jeske, is your church a gay-friendly congregation as some churches are?

A: My congregation is friendly to everybody, and that includes people who have knowingly and unknowingly sinned against God's commandments, people who may be actively in rebellion against God's will but who are looking for strength and truth. I know that some of the members and attenders of my congregation are same-sex oriented, and I am pretty sure that many more I don't know about feel the pull of same-sex attraction.

All sinners need to be in contact with the Word of God on a regular basis, for only the Word can change their lives. That includes homosexual sin, but liars, thieves, abusers, coveters, and heterosexual sinners need the Word too, and so we welcome them as well. *Welcoming people and being kind to them does not imply endorsement of their way of life.*

You can't believe the New Testament and condone the gay lifestyle. Romans chapter 1 and 1 Corinthians chapter 6 leave no room for that. But banning and shunning people doesn't help them—it only drives them farther into the gay world to find acceptance. Biblical Christians are sometimes smeared with the term *homophobic*, which is unjust. *Phobos* is the Greek word for fear—biblical Christians aren't afraid of gay people. We just don't think their lifestyle is spiritually healthy. It's not *my* opinion of people that matters—but it is my job to relay God's opinion, which is a matter of life and death.

When someone who is same-sex oriented wants to believe in Christ, he or she will face a lifestyle choice that will cost him or her. The Christian way will at times seem lonely and hard, and those people need a lot of love and encouragement to make up for what they are giving up. It may be that the only realistic life choice for them is to be single and celibate. How can you not celebrate someone who loves Jesus that much?

* * * * * * *

Q: If Paul says in 1 Corinthians chapter 7 that it's better to be single in the Lord than married because your interests are divided, then why do so many pastors and "men of God" get married?

A: You are quoting only part of 1 Corinthians chapter 7 (smile). See also verse 2, which says that because there is so much immorality, each man should have his own wife and each woman her own husband. First Corinthians chapter 7 is just one more example of the many paradoxes in the Word of God—Paul praises both the single life and the married life.

I have lived as a pastor in both worlds, and they both have much to commend about them. I was a single pastor for six years before God had mercy on me and allowed me to find a spouse. As a single guy I could work insane hours, come and go as I pleased, and focus all my energy on the church. Are those good things? You bet.

But in some ways I am even more valuable to my congregation as a married pastor. I now have a counselor who lives right in my home and gives me priceless advice. She explains to me the thought processes and behaviors of the other 50 percent of the human race. She teaches me things about manners and social interactions. Without her insights I would be much clumsier in serving the women in my congregation and community. I am a vastly better counselor to married couples now that I am a husband. I know the joys and difficulties of marriage from firsthand experience.

Singleness worked for St. Paul. But it doesn't work for everybody.

● ● ● ● ● ● ●

Q: My Reformed friends vehemently disagree with the right of Lutheran pastors to forgive sin, as it is declared in Lutheran Communion services. You have described Isaiah's quote of God's forgiveness of sin, that "he and only he" forgives sins. However, the Lutheran tradition "claims" Jesus' declaration of John chapter 20, in which Jesus tells (breathed upon) his disciples that they (we?) can forgive sins as well. Can you explain this?

A: I think this is really two discussions and perhaps involves a misunderstanding. The first concerns where the forgiveness of our sins comes from. There is absolutely nothing to argue about here—our forgiveness was purchased 100 percent by Jesus Christ. All the washing, all the justification, all the love, all the cleansing, all the atonement, all the righteousness come from him and his tremendous sacrifice on the cross. The only priest we need, the only go-between, is our Great High Priest himself. There are no human filters needed to broker that heavenly mercy.

The second point concerns how those concepts are shared. The message of God's mercy has been entrusted to all Christians (not just to pastors) to proclaim to the world, along with the call to repentance and warnings of God's wrath on those who refuse to repent. It's not *our* message; it's God's. We don't generate any of the content; we can't improve on the product; we just pass on the bad news of human sin and the good news of Jesus' atonement. All of God's royal priests do that on a personal basis; congregations elect worship leaders to speak for them when they gather in large groups publicly (i.e., pastors in worship services).

The intent of the language of the public confession of sins is not to make the pastor think he's God or to convince laypeople that they must go to an ordained pastor for assurance of their forgiveness. It is to encourage people to believe the wonderful gospel as though God were speaking it personally, as Jesus instructed in John chapter 20. When Jesus breathed on his disciples and empowered them to represent him, they still remained only the messengers. The ultimate Forgiver is still Jesus Christ alone.

* * * * * * *

Q: I struggle with the doctrine of fellowship. We are studying it in our church's Bible class. The doctrine states that we are to avoid participating in any "religious" activity with members of an organization that has teachings that are contrary to the Bible. That is very obvious to me. My problem is when doing this, I feel that I am sending a message that I/we/my church body is "better" than they. I have been told by our pastor that he feels that there will be people from all churches in heaven with us, but while on earth we must segregate ourselves from anyone not in full fellowship with our church body. I truly believe that we have a message to spread, and this doctrine seems to inhibit us in interacting with others. Please give me your guidance.

A: You have a nice way of expressing the dilemma. In a sense, Christians have to find the sweet spot between our intense concern for careful Bible study and teachings on the one hand and on the other hand both outreach with the Word and interaction with other Christians. We must not compromise or surrender what we know to be true from Scripture, but we want to show kindness, patience, and understanding with other Christians who weren't brought up the way we were or taught with the same religious vocabulary that we were.

All Christians, you and I included, shouldn't just repeat things we've heard from esteemed pastors and teachers of yesterday. We need to do our own Bible study and make our faith heritage our own. When we address differences of belief with friends, we need to quote Scripture, not the resolutions and documents of our church body or what we think we heard years ago.

All church bodies have to struggle with how and where to build their fences—how to distinguish truth from error, but also how to build those fences without insulting and disrespecting people from other tribes. All church bodies also have to struggle with what they absolutely will not tolerate among their pastors and teachers and where are the areas in which there can be a legitimate difference of opinion.

Scripture gives us strong encouragement in both directions—we are commanded to hold fast to the sure faith of God's Holy Word, but Jesus also told his disciples to show respect and kindness to sincere Christians who "were not one of them"(Luke 9:50). Relationships will always be messy. Knowing when to separate yourself and when to embrace is art, not science, and not everybody agrees on when and how to do either. Some Christian leaders take a harder edge on their fellowship practices; some are gentler and more tolerant.

St. Paul said it best: **"Speak the truth in love"** (Ephesians 4:15).

● ● ● ● ● ● ●

Q: In the Lord's Supper, is the bread and wine actually God's body and blood, or does it turn into his body and blood at some point during the Sacrament?

A: The scriptural accounts of the Lord's Supper are brief and will never answer all of the questions that our curiosity might wish. The gospel accounts of Matthew, Mark, and Luke each detail Jesus' institution of the Lord's Supper; Paul writes important information in 1 Corinthians chapters 10 and 11; and that's about it. This much is clear—Jesus promises that when people receive the Supper they are receiving his true body and blood along with the bread and wine. "This *is* my body. . . . This *is* my blood," he said. Holy Communion is the gospel of Christ right in our mouths, so that we cannot possibly mistake who is meant for the personal forgiveness of sins.

St. Paul tells us that in the Supper there is a holy union, a sacred *communion*, between bread and body and wine and blood (1 Corinthians 10:16). When unrepentant sinners in Corinth were eating and drinking of the Supper in an unworthy manner, they were **"sinning against the body and blood of the Lord"** (1 Corinthians 11:27).

Scripture teaches that when a Christian group gathers, brings bread and wine, the sacred words of Jesus are repeated, and people receive it, they are receiving Christ himself. There is not enough information in the brief scriptural accounts to make any assertions about the moment in time when ordinary bread and wine become the extraordinary sacrament. Various Christian scholars have made passionate arguments for the moment being when the pastor speaks the words of institution, and others equally protest that the moment is when the communicants receive it. But those are just hypotheses, not scriptural doctrine. If this question still matters to you on the day after judgment day, you can ask Jesus.

● ● ● ● ● ● ●

Q: My wife and I started attending a church in our area where there is an expectancy that everyone take Communion at every service they attend. I don't believe my salvation depends on taking Communion so often. Can you shed some light on my concerns about being expected to take Communion at every service?

A: There is no biblical commandment about how often you are supposed to receive the Sacrament. It is simply God's gift. Your salvation does not depend on the number of times you have communed, but on the pure mercy of Christ and your faith in him. Each congregation and its members have been given the freedom to organize their worship life as they see fit. There are no laws of the ceremonies as in Old Testament times. Congregations are free to choose the frequency and manner in which they will gather for the sacrament.

You also have personal freedom in these matters. Communion participation is not a law. Communion is a precious gift from God. You are a royal priest of God, in charge of your own spiritual care and feeding (1 Peter 2:9). You may decide, without pressure or bullying, when you choose to commune. Pastors should invite; they should never coerce. The Sacrament is a meal of grace, not a membership requirement or performance obligation.

If you choose not to commune every Sunday in a church culture that has every-Sunday Communion, perhaps it would be wise to have a quiet word with your pastor to explain your thoughts so he won't assume that you don't value the sacrament or think that you are staying away because you think you have unforgivable sins on your conscience. It would also show respect to the pastor to let him explain the rationale for every-Sunday Communion.

But the final decision on Communion attendance is yours.

3

*"As for me and my household, we will serve the L*ORD*"*
(Joshua 24:15).

Family Life and Marriage

Q: My husband and I have been trying to have another baby. Unfortunately four of my pregnancies ended up in miscarriages. We have not stopped believing that the Lord will bless us with a precious little boy. Should we keep trying or just give up? Is it God's holy will that I have another baby?

A: Infertility is one of the bitter burdens for the human race to bear ever since the fall into sin. It is one of many broken aspects of our existence this side of heaven. The Bible has many stories of the heartbreak of men and women with empty arms, men like Abraham and women like Hannah. As you share your stories of miscarriages with people close to you, you are probably hearing from many other women who too have had to endure the disappointment of a miscarriage.

Miscarriages are not your fault. God is not punishing you for any of your past sins small or great. They are just sad experiences that show us how broken everything on earth really is. Death has invaded every part of our world, even in the womb, the very place of the creation of human life. Perhaps God in his mercy knew that those four little ones would not have survived life outside the womb and so he took them into his arms early.

We will never know why some couples conceive so easily, why some people with no ability to care for a child are given children they barely want, and why Christian couples eager and willing to be parents should have to wait so long or be denied.

What I do know is this: infertility is common—you and your husband are not alone. By some estimates, 10 percent of men and 10 percent of women suffer physical limitations that make bringing a healthy baby to term very difficult or impossible. That means that perhaps one of every five couples in our country will have struggles like yours. This is not a punishment from God, nor God's negative opinion of your child-raising abilities. Our pain is his pain too, for he is our Father, and good fathers hurt when their children hurt.

My pastoral heart and counsel to you is to give God every opportunity to give you the child you dream of. I can't imagine how hard four miscarriages must be, but if you can stand the strain, go for it. One of my dearest friends, a former member of my congregation, didn't get married till she was 40, and she bore two amazing children. When our last child was born, my wife was 38 and I was a ripe old 42.

God puts children in our lives in many ways. He may keep that promise through natural childbirth, or maybe adoption, or maybe foster parenting, or maybe Sunday school teaching, or maybe . . . ? May God's marvelous promise in Psalm 113 come true in your life.

* * * * * * *

Q: My husband and I just had a baby and I really love being a mom, but I also want to go back to work. Is that wrong? Do you think God wants me to stay at home since he called me to be a mom?

A: One of the hardest life dilemmas of living in the 21st century is the decision that mothers of small children have to make—how soon to return to the workforce. When you are 80 years old, looking backward over your life, you will never regret a single minute of time that you chose to spend with your kids. This was not an issue for my grandmother— all moms of her generation were home with the kids. But labor-saving machines, technology, and husbands who help around the house have changed the equation. How blessed you are to have a husband with a job—you have a choice!

Ask yourself why you want to go back to work outside the home. Are you being crushed by debt and need the money that badly? Do you crave the approval of other working moms? Does a little voice in your head tell you that being a stay-at-home mom is a waste of your education? Are you afraid of losing time on the career ladder?

Another factor is the money that you will *net*. Do the math on both arrangements—how much of your salary would be burned up with childcare and transportation costs? How much extra money would you have to spend on prepared food or eating out because you wouldn't have time to cook? Who would care for a sick child? Some stay-at-home moms work it both ways—they make money watching other people's kids in their home and get to be with their own when they are small. Working moms can be great moms too. Is there possibly a grandparent who can provide some childcare for at least part of the week?

There isn't a clear right-or-wrong choice to make. If there were, God would have laid it all out in the Bible. But he didn't. Therefore you and your husband are entrusted with the choice, and your friends and family should respect what you come up with.

• • • • • • •

Q: Is it bad not to bring my kids to church? They get so loud and fussy! Can they even understand what's going on?

A: I feel a little sheepish commenting on having small children in church. Since I am a pastor, I am expected to sit up in front all by myself. My poor wife had to tend our four children all by herself. My first encouragement is always for parents to bring their children, even little ones, into the sanctuary. That's where they learn how to sit still. That's where they learn the words to the Lord's Prayer and Apostles' Creed. That's where they learn the magic of congregational singing. That's where they can watch the choirs and instrumentalists make music. That's where you can teach them about generosity and the giving of offerings to the Lord. That's where they can acquire an array of aunts and uncles in their church family. They might even get some usable fragments from the pastor's message that you can talk about on the way home.

Small children do indeed have short attention spans, and they do make noise. Here are some thoughts:

- Most churches have "cry rooms." Do not feel ashamed or inadequate as a parent if you take your kids there. Often. Our church has a room away from the sanctuary with church sound piped in so that the adults in the room can hear the message. There is a changing table and toys and books for small children. Some larger congregations even have staffed nurseries where you can take a toddler for part or all of the service.

- If your church's "cry room" doesn't exist or isn't furnished with any toys, consider volunteering to help organize one. If you really care about this issue, you could help organize a childcare co-op and take turns caring for each other's kids.

- Some wonderful people in our congregation built a little "quiet bag" tree near the sanctuary entrance. Parents of wee ones can pick up a bag, which has soft toys, a few books, and a coloring book and some crayons, and then return it after the service.

- Bring a baggie of cereal, the approved toddler church food for five straight decades. Give them one piece at a time.

- Don't be afraid to ask for a little help from other people. They might be glad to help you. You don't have to do this all by yourself. Some grandparents who live far from their grandkids might be delighted to hold a child for a little while.

- Try sitting near the front once in a while instead of in the back. Kids get a lot more out of the service when there aren't so many visual distractions in their way. Carol tells me that our kids were way better behaved when she sat near the front.

- Hang on and don't panic. Kids grow up so fast! Before you know it, they will be large, moody teenagers and you will be willing to pay any amount of money to have them little again.

- Ignore the glares and be proud of your role in building a future for your congregation. A church without little kids running around is probably dying.

• • • • • • •

Q: How do I balance encouraging my 12-year-old to do her best without pushing her to perfectionism? She always tells me, "You expect me to be perfect!"

A: The trick is to figure out where setting high goals ends and perfectionism begins. How can you tell the difference? High goals are good. Never let a culture develop in your home where half-jobs, mediocrity, and sloppy work are tolerated. Kids will always push back against any parental expectations, probing for weakness, inconsistency, guilt, and lack of parental follow-through. Just because your child accuses you of perfectionism doesn't mean that you are guilty of it.

But you do need to check yourself for it. Perfectionism is destructive because perfectionist parents

- Never praise their children.

- Keep their children guessing as to whether they approve of them or not.

- Try to push their kids to be clones of themselves instead of letting the children's own skills, interests, and talents emerge.

- Constantly compare their kids to other kids who are high achievers and only praise the other kids.

- Make their kids feel that nothing is ever good enough.

- Overuse the phrase, "When I was your age . . ."

- Use guilt as a motivator.

- Fail to praise and encourage children in the beginning stages of sports or music lessons and thus make them feel permanently incompetent, discouraging them from sticking to it

- Never stop—they keep the doubt and fear and guilt going even when they are 75 and their kid is 55.

Child raising is messy. You may never feel as though you got that balance right (I sure don't). I remember making one of my kids cry as I harangued him to practice the piano harder. I also am not real proud that I let my kids let some things slide that they should have taken care of. In Christ we are forgiven of our parenting sins too.

So repent of your weaknesses and shortcomings, and then go back and work on being a great parent. Look for something to praise in each of your kids today. Let them know for sure how proud you are of them (I don't care what age they are). And thank God that he entrusted you with these precious human beings.

● ● ● ● ● ● ● ●

Q: I'm a stay-at-home mom of three kids under 5. How can I find joy in the everyday tasks of changing diapers and picking up toys? I'm always tired and don't feel like I'm making a real difference in the world.

A: I'm not going to shame you or guilt you for feeling that way. A parent of a very small child is basically that child's slave—the child's needs trump everything else that the parent might like to do. Keeping them alive, safe, fed, stimulated, educated, and clean will leave anyone exhausted by 6:30 P.M. And then you have to get up the next day and do it again. *Times three.* You will go through long stretches of time when you wonder, "When is somebody going to do something for *me*?!" My wife used to go stir crazy just for another adult to talk to during the day.

When Jesus told his disciples that the greatest in God's

kingdom were those who served the most, he was probably thinking of mothers of small children first. If the King of kings and Lord of lords could wash his disciples' feet, you can choose to find joy in changing diapers, since we know how pleasing this service is to the Lord. It is actually a series of acts of worship that you get to do in your "church" (i.e., home).

The time you spend with your preschoolers will have an enormous impact on their academic success. The literacy skills you give them—reading to them, teaching them to love books and enjoy learning their letters and numbers— will set them up for success in all grades later on. The time you spend with your preschoolers reading Bible stories and singing Christian songs will help their newly planted faith to grow stronger to resist the evil one.

● ● ● ● ● ● ●

Q: I'm often impatient with my kids. I pray for patience daily, but I'm worried that the damage is done and they will grow up to be as crabby and impatient with their children as I have been with them. What can I do?

A: The first thing you can do is praise God that he has given you the precious gift of self-awareness. Your situation is vastly better than one in which the verbally abusive parent is unaware of the damage she is doing.

Second, ask for help from the children's father (that would be true whether you are married or unmarried). Men are often afraid of a woman's temper and tongue and run for cover when mom is "going off." Allow this important man in your life to whisper to you when your tongue is getting too sharp. Ask for his feedback if your dialogue with your kids is inappropriate. Give him permission to intervene and rein you in if he feels that you are losing your temper.

Third, do a little personal inventory. Why is it that you are so crabby? Do you like yourself? Are you proud of your life's accomplishments? Do you feel encouraged and supported and admired by the children's father? Do you carry around a lot of guilt? Was your own mother harsh or judgmental or perfectionistic? Do you think you suffer from depression? I know dozens of people in my congregation who use antidepressants to regulate their mood swings. I'm not pushing greater drug use on people, but it is an option for you to consider.

Fourth, bask personally in God's unconditional love for you, and then you will have unconditional love to give. Appreciate God's patience with a work in progress like you, and you will have more patience for others. Celebrate God's rich load of blessings on your life, and you won't feel so panicky that the wheels are coming off all the time. Intentionally look for things to praise in your kids and shock them with words of encouragement and praise *just because*.

Fifth, have the bigness of spirit to apologize to the kids when you know you've been out of line. Parents are often terrified of ever showing weakness to the kids, fearing that everything will unravel. It won't. In fact, it will make you more human and approachable. Kids need not only to hear "sermons" about how they should apologize—they should also see their parents do it and model it for them. They won't respect you any less; in fact, they will probably respect and appreciate you more.

* * * * * * *

Q: At what age do you think we should allow our children to date? And how should we prepare them?

A: Two mighty questions. If you have girls, these important decisions will come up first with them. Girls seem to me to mature faster than boys; girls are more interested in relationships than boys; and from time immemorial boys will often seek to date girls younger than they and only seldom does the reverse happen.

Girls are more vulnerable. I say that not as a chauvinist (I hope) but as a dad. I am also a recovering male teenager with fairly clear memories of what I was like from ages 18 to 24. If I was going to err as a dad with my rules, I always want to err on the side of caution rather than too much liberty.

We had a general rule in our house that you had to be 16 before you could start dating, and we preferred group dates first. We wanted to know where they were at all times. We watched intently for signs that she could be trusted: Did she listen respectfully to our instructions? Did she keep her promises? Was she back on time? Did we ever catch her in deceptions or lies? Were there sudden changes in arrangements halfway through the evening? As she grew in our trust, we let the reins go a little more.

In her junior and senior years of high school, we would allow single dates on special occasions. We wanted to meet the young man and know about his family. We wanted to see him up close and have him look into our eyes—just a little reminder that she was not an independent agent in life or his personal game but that she was connected to a family that *cared*. Once they go off to college, you better have laid down a good pattern, because now they are completely on their own (smile).

The prepping speech is to help them appreciate the strong, even violent forces that drive our lives. First, reminding them of the awesomely destructive power of the automobile. When my boys wanted to borrow the car, I remember often referring to it as the "2,000 lb. killing machine." Second, counseling the boys about respecting the girls, respecting her family, and respecting their rules. Third, counseling our daughter about the enormously powerful sex drive that influences the behaviors of all males, especially the young ones, a force that can lead even nice guys to do stupid and selfish things. Finally, warning them about the destructive power of alcohol.

We tried to make our home a place where our kids and their friends of both genders felt comfortable hanging out. I would rather have them here than out on the streets.

● ● ● ● ● ● ●

Q: How can I deal with my teenage son? He is so disrespectful! I need God's help to transform my family.

A: Here is a universal cry of agony from a Christian who sees an angry and rebellious child. This happens all the time, and it happens all over. In fact, hardly any family has escaped times of serious pushback from a child. What do you do when you're that parent or grandparent and you see not only that kind of anger and attitude against you personally but then have to hear derisive remarks from them about the Christian faith and the church?

Step one: try to understand where that anger is coming from. Some kids are busy trying on various masks and faces to find out who they are. It may be a phase. Some kids have been hurt deeply by traumas in their lives, and they are lashing back at you not necessarily because of anything you have done but because you're there. You're the only convenient target. Is his dad in his life? Some boys with absent fathers feel betrayed and cheated their whole lives, and since they can't fight with the missing dad, they take out their bitterness on the mother. Even teenage boys with a dad at home will test their strength, and usually they pick on Mom first because they see her tenderness as weakness that they despise.

Step two: listen. If you just go ballistic or get upset, all that does is feed the negativity that's going on inside this young person. It's important that you show that you are trying to understand things from the teen's point of view. I like to think I am the world's greatest listener, but I have vivid memories of one of my teenage boys shouting at me, "You never listen to me."

Step three: show unconditional love. "I'm never going to shun you. I'm not going to shame you. I'm not going to mock you." By the time kids get to the teen years, they know how to push your buttons, and it's important that you control your own anger so that you don't say things you later regret. Always give all your kids a steady diet of words that affirm how valuable you see them and how precious they are to you.

Step four: your kids are not your buddies or equals, no matter how big they get. Don't beg them for good behavior. Don't offer bribes. State what you think is appropriate for them and then insist that you are listened to. Don't expect that your tears will melt their hearts. Immature young men see tears only as weakness, which they despise. Your will has to be stronger than his.

Step five: network with other parents in your situation and share insights and tactics.

Step six: pray. Pray, and bring him to church. It's really hard to stay mad at someone who is sitting next to you and singing with you.

● ● ● ● ● ● ●

Q: My daughter is going off to college this year. I feel like we've done our best as parents, but I'm worried she'll be sucked into partying and drinking and sex. I know you've sent kids to college—any advice?

A: Now you know how God feels (smile). After all the guidance, care, education, and generosity, now we hold our breath to see what kind of adults our kids will be. They have to make their own choices, just as God waits and watches to see what we will do with our lives.

It may come as a comfort to you to know that there's nothing you can do at this point. Your work is mostly done. At age 18 our kids aren't listening to us much anymore— their friends are now their main advisors. You can help her by locating the nearest church that you think would be good for her and by tracking down information on campus ministries of your denomination. Call the ministry office yourself and let them know how to find your daughter. The first month away from home can be pretty lonely, and some love from a familiar worshiping group might really resonate.

If you have worries that you can't shake, have The Talk with her. Tell her plainly (and briefly) what you worry about and why. If you keep it short, and if you treat her like the adult she now thinks she is, she will remember what you say (even if protesting her maturity and seeming to blow you off). She will be quietly glad that you care about her that much. Find out (through websites and maybe some phone

calls) about the security services that her campus provides—
many colleges offer late-night library shuttle buses,
emergency phone numbers, parking lot security
attendants, etc.

And then give her to Jesus and let go. Your prayers will
keep her needs in front of God's throne, and his angels will
hover over her. You have given her roots; now she gets to try
out her wings.

● ● ● ● ● ● ●

Q: Proverbs 22:6 says, **"Start children off on the way they
should go, and even when they are old they will not turn
from it."** I feel like I raised my children in faith, but now
none of them go to church and my son says he's agnostic.
What did I do wrong? What do I do now?

A: The very same Scriptures that tell us that wonderful
proverb also narrate the story of the prodigal son. Do you
suppose that the father in Jesus' parable was a terrible
spiritual leader in his home? I bet not. I bet he was a great
dad. The boy just had a streak of wildness and selfishness.
Samuel and David, two of the greatest heroes in all Bible
history, both had some terrible sons who disgraced both
their fathers and their faith. Don't beat on yourself too
hard—you tried your best to bring up your children in the
training and instruction of the Lord.

You can't believe for your children. You gave them the
words of spiritual life. They now know the truth of the
gospel. The Bible's core teachings are in their minds and
hearts, waiting to be grasped and believed and lived. So now
we wait.

It is important to control your fear and impatience and

play a long game now. God can use many tools over the long haul to show people that there is no forgiveness of sins, no inner peace, and no heaven without Jesus Christ. Just as alcoholics have to bottom out before they are ready to listen and change, God may have to let your prodigals run for a long time and find for themselves the hollowness of Satan's lies. He may use his divine two-by-four to get their attention when he thinks they're ready.

The prodigal son eventually grew up and came to his senses. I have seen that often in my own ministry—older people coming back to church after decades of wandering. Yesterday I sat on the couch of a 76-year-old regular visitor to my congregation who told me of how much he enjoys the services after 50 years of never going to church. I once baptized a 72-year-old man in the hospital just a few days before he died—God loved him all those years and wouldn't let go until he repented.

Never stop loving your kids. Never shun them. Never shame them. Always show respect. Treat them as adults, no matter how juvenile and foolish you think their words and actions are. Speak words of Jesus' gospel—only the gospel converts. And pray like crazy.

* * * * * * *

Q: I have two cousins (one on each side of the family) who were both raised in Christian homes, but one was in jail for drugs and one is in prison for molesting his daughters. How do I support their parents? I'm at a loss for words.

A: First, just hanging out with those parents will mean a great deal. Some of their friends and relatives may be avoiding them, and you can show that you still appreciate and value them. Their shame will be through the roof, and you can listen to their grief and help them bear it. You don't have to keep bringing it up or go digging for more and more sensational details, but you can be ready to talk about things when they are. They are probably feeling judged by their relatives and neighbors, and you can show acceptance and love in their time of misery.

You can also give the family comfort by visiting the cousins in prison (if geographically possible). You can show that you still consider them valuable human beings and give them hope of God's forgiveness and strength for the work of restoration that lies ahead. Clearly they were living unchristian lives, but perhaps God has now busted them down far enough that they are humbled and ready to listen to the Word.

Someday the cousins will be released. One of the great things about Christianity is that there can be next acts. God cares much more about our future than about our broken past. You can help your relatives prepare for the day when these men are released. If Jesus pardoned the criminal on the cross next to him, we can certainly forgive those who have sinned against us.

● ● ● ● ● ● ●

Q: I'm a single parent to three daughters. It's really hard. Does the Bible say anything about raising children on your own?

A: There aren't many Scripture references to single parenting, probably because the lot of a single parent back then was so bleak that young women and their families were much more afraid of it. There was no real governmental social safety net of any kind (partly because for much of Israel's history there was no government per se). Young men also knew that the wrath of the girl's father (and brothers) would come down on their heads if they created a fatherless grandchild.

There must have been plenty of single moms in Old Testament times, though, because of the near-constant warfare the people of Israel experienced. From the time of the exodus from Egypt until the Babylonian captivity, there would have been a constant supply of war widows, many of whom had children. The Law of Moses commanded that tithes of the harvest should be gathered and kept in common so that the foreigner, widow, and orphan could eat (Deuteronomy 14:29).

A parent can be forced to go solo because of death of a spouse, separation, divorce, or because the never-married partner left. But even with all the government services available to single parents today, the job is so hard that it's a wonder so many young people so casually flirt with it.

As a single parent, you will almost certainly carry a heavier load of fatigue, exhaustion, loneliness, regrets, guilt, and anger than a married parent (that's not to say that marriage is easy—married people have their own burdens to bear). You will be all the more grateful to hear the Lord's promise that he will meet all your needs through the glorious riches of Christ Jesus (Philippians 4:19). The peace and rest for your soul that Jesus promises in Matthew 11:28 is welcome news indeed.

Have you ever read the story of the single mom named Hagar? She was one of Abraham's maidservants and she conceived and bore his child (see Genesis 16 and Genesis 21:8-21). Abraham's wife, Sarah, at first supported the plan—the adultery was *intentional* and planned—but then she turned furiously on Hagar and compelled Abraham to drive her away from the family.

But God cared deeply for the lonely woman and her little boy. He appeared to her twice, the first time to name her son. God himself arranged that the boy would be called Ishmael, i.e., "God hears." Single moms should know that God hears their cries for help. Second, God intervened to sustain the lives of the two refugees and promised to *pour* out his blessings on Ishmael. Although Ishmael would not be the son of promise of the Israelite nation, he would found a nation of his own. All the Arab peoples today regard Ishmael as their father; ironically they vastly outnumber people of Jewish descent today.

So even if your family life is not turning out according to your original plan, call out to God, expect his providing, and open your eyes to new adventures by which you can serve him.

* * * * * * *

Q: I grew up in a home where my parents were very critical of me and my siblings. Now as a parent, I find myself repeating some of those tendencies to my children and not building them up as much as I'd like. How can I work to be more encouraging of them even when it's ingrained in my head to be critical?

A: I hear you, my friend. My own father would often quasi-apologize to my girlfriend and now wife, "We are very critical in our family." He said it with a smile, but I think he was both apologizing and repenting. He knew that his drive to do his best, and his drive for us to do our best, made him overly sharp-tongued sometimes and very critical of other people and their work. I am like him a lot and susceptible to those same weaknesses.

You are already in a good place, however, because you are aware of your tendency and you know the damage it can do. Invite your spouse to watch and listen for hypercriticism in your talk and tone. Be humble enough to let him or her tell you the truth about how you sound. We all often blurt things out through carelessness. Think before you talk, especially when you are upset or disappointed.

Realize that you can praise people into good behaviors more effectively than you can shame or criticize people out of bad behaviors. Your kids will want to grow into your praise more joyfully than cringe in shame from your disapproval and disappointment. If you look for things to praise in them, you will always find them. (If you look for failings in them, you will always find those things too.)

Maybe we're critical because deep down inside we don't like ourselves very much. Take inventory of the treasures in your life and see how richly blessed you are. Do you feel rich? Do you feel prosperous? Do you feel blessed? If you check in with God's Word, you will be looking at your life from a position of strength and abundance instead of a position of scarcity. And as you feel secure and good about your life—not that you're such an overachiever, but that God is so good to you—you will then have strength to be kind and patient to other people.

Treat your kids the way God treats you: with high expectations, forgiveness, encouragement, unconditional love, patience, help, guidance, role modeling, and a servant spirit. Have the grace to apologize when you catch yourself lapsing back into your old sharp-tongued ways. Ask God for forgiveness of your past excesses, and then assume and live in that forgiveness! Sins gone! Old me is gone and the new me is alive right now! Ask God for an encouraging tongue, *and he will give it to you.*

• • • • • • •

Q: Why did God create families?

A: He wouldn't have had to, I suppose. Being God, he could have designed the human experience any way he wanted. He didn't have to create gender. He could have figured out a way for the human species to reproduce without it. He could have designed a way for people to have a relationship with him completely apart from other people. But he didn't do any of those things.

He created two humans in his image—loving him, loving good, loving each other. He had started with just the male, but only hours later he announced that **"it is not good for the man to be alone"** (Genesis 2:18). He arranged that only together would human reproduction be possible. He decided that Adam and Eve's birthday would also be their wedding day and joined them together. He intended marriage to be a bonding force stronger than that between a person and his or her parents.

God is intensely social. He derives huge satisfaction from loving his children and being loved by them. How would he not create people to be just like him? He designed the growth and development process to be pretty long—it's two decades before an infant is regarded as a full-grown adult. Families can protect and socialize their young in a remarkably efficient way.

It's also a powerful form of evangelism. Families serve

as the primary way in which the Word of God is passed to the next generation. I would guess that the majority of Christians first learned about Jesus from their father, or more likely their mother.

None of this is to say that single people aren't useful to God's plan. They themselves are the product of a family and have an important network of relatives. There are many other human networks, including congregations especially, which function as spiritual families where single people can use their gifts, grow in their faith, and serve others. Even though God could have found other ways to get all of this done, I think what he came up with is pretty cool.

● ● ● ● ● ● ●

Q: Why does God want some people to be alone while others marry and seem to have no trouble meeting other people?

A: Why do things happen? Does everything happen because God has ordained it so? Do *we* make things happen and God watches? Or is it some mixture of the above? The correct answer is "C."

Stuff happens both because of what God has ordained and willed, but also because of our choices. Our personalities, our philosophies of how we operate, our vocabulary, the decisions that we make really do matter. The only person who can tell where God's actions and choices leave off and ours begin is God himself. The Bible tells us that he does step in and makes certain things happen, but other things we choose, and we carry the responsibility for the decisions that we make. We will never know completely where the one starts and the other leaves off.

Is it possible that God has chosen someone to serve him in a single life and kind of arranges that that person will be single his or her whole life? Yes. Do we want to leave room that that is something God may have ordained? Sure. But we shouldn't assume because someone is single that God did it. Someone who desperately wants to be married shouldn't say, "God, why are you preventing me from getting married?" You don't know that.

The Bible also tells us not to get too hyper about our situation in life. Everyone would like to have great finances and prosperity, but sometimes we are honoring God while we are in our poor time of life, when we're really broke and have nothing. St. Paul said, **"I have learned to be content whatever the circumstances. I know what it is to be in need, and I know what it is to have plenty. I have learned the secret of being content in any and every situation. . . . I can do all this through him who gives me strength"** (Philippians 4:11-13).

That same attitude will sustain you in your love life. The Bible tells us that living a single life is not a curse; in fact, it's a huge blessing. St. Paul wrote, **"I wish that all of you were as I am** (i.e., single). **. . . Those who marry will face many troubles in this life, and I want to spare you this"** (1 Corinthians 7:7,28). But in that same chapter he also says that because there is so much immorality in the world, each man should have a wife and vice versa. At this point you might interrupt, "He just contradicted himself!" Well, let's call it a paradox—both statements are true. Both the single state and the married state are potentially great ways to live in order to serve the Lord.

If you know somebody who's frustrated by being single— and I hasten to add you may also know some people who are married and are wishing or are even acting as though they were single—encourage people to find the joy in their lives right now. But we can also pray with singles that God would grant things they earnestly desire in their hearts, and perhaps those prayers will set romantic things in motion. It's been my personal joy to have dear friends who got married in their thirties, forties, even sixties. Never say "Game Over" to God. He's full of surprises.

Does God *want* certain people to be married and some to be single? We'll never unravel that puzzle ourselves. Let me just encourage you to enjoy your life where you're at right now. Be the best single person you can be. If you'd like to be married, keep your eyes open, go to places where single people hang out, make friends, and don't ever brush off blind dates—some great marriages happen from blind dates! Enjoy the people whom God sends into your life. Keep your eyes open for what he just might wish to do to bless you.

● ● ● ● ● ● ●

Q: Can you commit adultery if you're not married?

A: Yes. There is a little confusion over the Bible's sexual instructions because the two primary words used for sexual sin in the Greek New Testament, *moicheia* and *porneia*, are used in the New Testament in both a wider and narrower sense, and the context has to help you identify the precise meaning. Both can refer in a general sense to all sexual sin.

Moicheia's more specific meaning is sexual activity between a married man and another woman or between a married woman and another man. In other words, the basic evil of the sin is compounded by marital infidelity, which can lead to breakup of the marriage. Sometimes the usual

English translation of the word *adultery* is intended to refer only to marital sexual infidelity. In the Sixth Commandment (Exodus 20:14), however, "committing adultery" condemns all sexual sin, whether the adulterer is married or not. There the word is used in the general sense.

Porneia's specific meaning is sexual activity between two unmarried persons. Its English equivalent is the slightly antique-sounding word *fornication*, a word fading from contemporary usage, just as the social stigma of "shacking up" is fading away.

So here's the question: is fornication a sin? Yes. Listen to these words from the Word:

· **"Among you there must not be even a hint of sexual immorality, or of any kind of impurity"** (Ephesians 5:3).

· **"It is God's will that you should be sanctified: that you should avoid sexual immorality; that each of you should learn to control your own body in a way that is holy and honorable, not in passionate lust like the pagans, who do not know God"** (1 Thessalonians 4:3-5).

· **"Of this you can be sure: No immoral person** [in Greek, *pornos*, fornicator] **. . . has any inheritance in the kingdom of Christ and of God"** (Ephesians 5:5).

· **"You have heard that it was said, 'You shall not commit adultery.' But I tell you that anyone who looks at a woman lustfully has already committed adultery with her in his heart"** (Matthew 5:27,28).

In my opinion, our culture's casual toleration and even embrace of premarital (and extramarital) sexual behaviors are eroding our national ability to want to be married and to stay faithfully married. The steady increase of the percentage of children born each year out of wedlock is a national time bomb whose destructive effects we are only beginning to experience. Please join with me in holding up and respecting God's beautiful design for the most precious of all human relationships.

● ● ● ● ● ● ●

Q: With all the murder, theft, arson, and so on going on, do you really think God cares about cohabitation? This isn't the 1950s.

A: A sassy question, but I don't mind, because you have articulated what many think today.

Does God care about cohabitation? Indeed he does. Kindly see my response to the previous questioner and the Scripture references. God designed sexual intimacy to be the exciting glue that helps sustain the love and commitment between a man and woman who have publicly and permanently committed themselves to each other.

God's principles are timeless. He doesn't think in terms of decades but millennia. His commandments are not subject to public referenda. In our country we make, amend, and repeal our own laws. God's are beyond our editing. His ancient penalties for rebellion are still in force. His great wisdom and kindly Fatherly heart still breathe personal human benefit to us as we find that our lives are really way better when we keep his commandments. They are there to help us, not smother our freedom and creativity. He invented his rules about human sexuality to strengthen and protect family life, not cheat you out of adult fun that you think you have a right to.

The 1950s in some ways were a worse time to live in America. Jim Crow laws still made black folks live and feel like second-class citizens. Women's workplace and business skills were not generally appreciated or rewarded. But there was a far higher percentage of intact families, including among minority communities. The number of children in crisis was a tiny percentage of the epidemic of today. A friend of mine who works as a social services supervisor calls life in America's cities today a "trauma culture." The army of fatherless boys and girls grows by the day because we are losing both our desire for marriage and our ability to commit to one partner.

I believe, in fact, that God cares about human sexual behaviors if anything even more today than ever. If we had stronger and more stable marriages and homes, there would be less arson, theft, and murder.

● ● ● ● ● ● ●

Q: I have two nephews who are expecting babies with their girlfriends, and they refuse to get married. One is for financial reasons because then he would have to pay more alimony/child support to his first wife, and the other is simply because he is not a Christian and I'm assuming his girlfriend is not either. I do not want to support these two nephews because they are not doing what is pleasing to God, so when it comes around for baby showers and gifts for these two babies, do I just not attend or give gifts?

A: You have elegantly articulated the dilemmas of how Christians have to try to navigate the turbulent waters of an increasingly non-Christian culture and social climate in our world today.

I have heard the financial excuses made by cohabiters. If you have no Christ in you, they make perfect sense. They are just business decisions to lower overhead. I've even heard the same line of thought used by cohabiting retirees who are afraid of having their benefits reduced if they get married.

If there is no Christ in a person's heart, if the Bible has no hold on people's consciences or behaviors, no amount of persuasion or arguing is going to move them toward a Christ-centered solution that they think will cost them something significant. You can't change another person. Only people can change their own behaviors. Your only strategy, therefore, is to see if the Word of God has any pull with your two nephews. If it does, do your homework and work through the Bible passages with them. If they don't, you are wasting your breath (at least for now).

If they are motivated by Christ and his Word at all, assure them that God will always, *always* make a way for his people when they choose to make sacrifices of obedience to him. Financial fear is just a trick of Satan's to keep people thinking that God is not involved in their lives. Faithfulness to God and alignment with his life principles over time builds financial security, not loss.

As to the dilemma of participating in family activities with people who are not living a godly lifestyle: in my view, your attending an event—wedding, shower, anniversary— and the giving of gifts *do not automatically constitute an endorsement of their lifestyle* (disclaimer: I know that there are some Christian pastors who disagree with me on that). I don't believe that shaming and shunning work—they only make people angry, make them more determined than ever to continue in their wrong actions, and find their acceptance from people with similar lifestyles. In the future they will listen to you even less. If God can love sinners unconditionally, so can we.

I see it as a form of long-range evangelism to stay engaged with all of your family. They may not be listening right now, but since all of Satan's substitutes for God's life patterns cause pain and brokenness over time, they may come to realize that you were right. If you stick around, they may listen later, even if not right now.

● ● ● ● ● ● ●

Q: My daughter just got married. They didn't live together beforehand (which I was proud of), but she says there hasn't been a "honeymoon phase" and that these first six months have been really hard. How do I encourage her?

A: Did you see this coming? Did you share your misgivings with your daughter? Or are you surprised and disappointed too?

No matter how carefully you date, no matter how much you think you can learn from your beloved's family background, you never know everything about a person. Day-to-day living reveals so much more about the true nature of spouses, as they let their guard down, show their true thoughts and character, and stop working so hard to put on a dating facade.

It's a good sign that your daughter has confided in you. Far worse would be if she kept pretending in front of you and bottled up her unhappiness. What you can do is work through the details of your daughter's struggles with her. Help her work out a strategy for getting her husband to change his bad behaviors, help her know how to sort through what's critical and what she can let slide. We never get 100 percent of what we dream of in a spouse, and building a happy marriage means that there are certain things in our spouses that we just decide to tolerate cheerfully, knowing that they may never change.

But listen in her stories for areas where you think she may be in the wrong. Her behavior and expectations might be adding to the problem, and she could use your maturity and experience to tell her what you have learned about marriage.

When two people are together in their faith in the Lord, when both worship the same Savior and accept the power and authority of his Word, anything is possible. Any conflict can be resolved by people who embrace scriptural words like these: **"Clothe yourselves with compassion, kindness, humility, gentleness and patience. Bear with each other and forgive one another if any of you has a grievance against someone. Forgive as the Lord forgave you"** (Colossians 3:12,13).

If the struggles persist, encourage her to seek prayer and counsel from her pastor. If they still continue, encourage her with her husband to seek professional Christian marital counseling. Those dear and helpful people have pretty much seen it all and can lay out a path to healing and reconciliation.

* * * * * * *

Q: Could you explain 1 Corinthians 7:4 to me about the wife's body belonging to the husband?

A: The Holy Spirit revealed some powerful and insightful ideas about marriage to his traveling bachelor evangelist. Though Paul never had a wife, his teachings bring important instruction from God on how to make this relationship work.

It's not too hard to wreck a marriage. As immature and

sinful newlyweds struggle to get control over their lives and get the other person to do what they want, they jockey for power in the home. A man might be tempted to use his bigger body and more powerful musculature to dominate and intimidate the woman into doing what he wants. The woman might use her sharp tongue and withholding of sex as a way to get what she wants. None of these things has any place in a Christian home. They are poisonous.

The entire 7th chapter of 1 Corinthians is full of marriage wisdom. Verse 4 is a good example: **"The wife does not have authority over her own body but yields it to her husband."** When a couple enters into a Christian marriage, they enter a solemn covenant to think in terms of "we," no longer "me." They agree to become each other's *servants*, willing to spend time and energy meeting each other's needs. This principle applies to men too: **"In the same way, the husband does not have authority over his own body but yields it to his wife"** (1 Corinthians 7:4). In a happy home there's no demanding or maneuvering—there is just asking, giving, and serving.

A happy marriage is one of surrender and trust. Each spouse is willing to respond to the requests of the other, trusting that he or she won't be taken advantage of. Godly wives don't use sex as a weapon; godly husbands study their wives, listen carefully to what they say, and use their unique gifts to make their wives' lives secure and fulfilled. In a happy Christian marriage, the spouses trust God too—they trust that by making themselves vulnerable to each other they won't be hurt. If God is asking them to risk this kind of servanthood, they trust that he will bless it.

In my opinion, men typically face greater temptations than do women when it comes to lust, pornography, infidelity, and other sexual sins. If men's and women's sex drives were exactly equal, prostitution would disappear overnight. A Christian DJ was talking on the radio about her sense of amazement at what she was discovering about her newlywed husband. "I couldn't believe it—he's, like, 'on' all the time." Just so.

But that doesn't give men a free pass to make excuses for immoral, fantasizing behavior. God gave women enormous power in their sexuality. The pornography, strip club, and sex industries use that power to capture and destroy men. A Christian woman can use it to build a stronger relationship with her husband and help him fight off Satan's temptations. Wives, we need you!

● ● ● ● ● ● ●

Q: Every time I try to talk to my wife about Jesus, she totally shuts me down. I'm afraid to mention anything anymore, but I'm even more afraid that I won't see her in heaven someday.

A: I think even God himself is baffled about what people find so repugnant in the gospel. What's not to like about the forgiveness of sins, prayer access to heaven itself, steady love and blessings throughout life, and the promise of immortality?

You are discovering that no one can believe for another. You may never know for sure what is keeping your wife from faith in Christ. You won't ever know for sure what she's really thinking. All you can do is provide the information about Christ that she needs, and then you have to let go and let the Holy Spirit do his work.

Wait for your right times. People don't want you coming

at them as though you're a salesperson hustling something or pushing something they don't want. Earn the right to be listened to, and one of the ways that you do that is by showing a listening ear to what's important to her. When you have invested serious time hearing out her issues, even when they're stressful to you or sometimes even critical of you, you can say, "Dear, I listened to everything you said. Now I need you to listen to what I'm going to say."

Keep it short. Do your homework. Know how to summarize the gospel message in a brief way; don't go on and on and on. Speak with respect. Don't push, shame, threaten, or ridicule. Show that your motivation for speaking is love, not the desire to bully someone else into your philosophy. Let her know that you love her so much you would like the relationship to be able to go on into eternity.

Keep the heart of your little message the unconditional love and grace of God. She has a Savior who loves her so much that he gave his life to bear the blow. Deep down inside she knows there's a God. Deep down inside she feels the guilt of unforgiven sin. Deep down inside she knows (and fears) you're right. Don't force a decision or any changes in behavior. Just ask her to hear you out. And then give it a rest and trust in the power of the Word. The Word will either do it or it won't. It's not on you.

● ● ● ● ● ● ●

Q: My husband and I are getting divorced, but I don't want a divorce; I still love him although he was abusive. How do I let him go? He has moved on too. He has a girlfriend and a pattern of hitting and hurting women. He is verbally and mentally abusive too.

A: My heart goes out to you, my dear. You love him still in spite of all his bad behaviors. But I think there are some pretty powerful signals that it's time for you to let him go and to ask for God's help in detaching. Are you in love with him, or are you in love with the concept of marriage?

First, he does not appear to want to be committed to you any longer. You can only do a marriage when two people want to do it together. One person, no matter how strong, no matter how loving, cannot sustain a relationship. It has to be committed to by both parties. If he is serious about pursuing another woman, he is showing that he doesn't want to change himself to reconnect with you. Perhaps he blames you for the divorce.

Second, the fact that he still exhibits patterns of abusive and violent behavior means that he hasn't learned to master and control those urges. Your loneliness may be romanticizing the good times you had with him and suppressing the days of fear and hurt. If he doesn't accept responsibility for his patterns of violence toward females, that only encourages him to stay in those nasty habits.

My counsel is to move on and ask God to help you meet somebody new. Until he ends the relationship with the other woman, comes to you with apologies and an acceptance of responsibility for his abuse, and then willingly submits to professional counseling, attempts at resuming your marriage could just hurt you even worse than you are now.

• • • • • • •

Q: I just found out that my spouse of nearly 19 years has been in a relationship with another woman for several months. He claims that although there was hugging and kissing, there was no sex. This is still adultery, isn't it? This is the second time that this has happened to me. I know that the Lord can forgive and that I should forgive too, but the details are only emerging after I press him hard for additional information. How can I stay married?

A: What a heartbreaking story and yet one all too common.

He *says* that there was no outright physical sexual adultery. That may well be true, but if he has lied to you and been evasive, it makes it hard for you to trust anything he says 100 percent. If you had to dig the information out of him bit by bit, you have no idea how much more there could be. Along with whatever you've scraped up, there's probably quite a bit more beneath the surface. The emotional dysfunction has probably been going on in one way or another for a long time.

Jesus said that a man who gazes lustfully on a woman has committed adultery with her in his heart, and so what your husband did is indeed a form of adultery. He has some serious repenting to do. He has massively disrespected you, shamed you before this other woman, and given you a wound in your heart that may never fully heal. Even if you choose to give him the benefit of the doubt and assume that there was no intercourse, the emotional infidelity is real. He took his loyalty and attention away from you and gave it to her. (She's just as much at fault in this as he, by the way).

I would definitely suggest a referee, a third party, someone whom you both will trust. I hope with your pastor or a marriage counselor that you will dig into the issues and be honest with each other. He gets a say too. Perhaps he has issues with things you've said or done, or not done, that you will have to listen to as well. If so, you can do your own repenting.

Your pastor can set a course of restoration for your

husband, and your husband's response will show to what degree he has humbled himself and wants to work to restore the relationship. Your pastor can also listen to your tone and advise you how to respond. If your husband's repentance is genuine, you can assure him of your forgiveness.

This event is a major blow to your marriage and needs to be addressed very seriously. But have hope. When two people in Christ come before him in repentance and faith, listening to his Word, and open to guidance, miracles can happen. Some dear friends of mine overcame an incident of actual adultery and are happily married still, 15 years later. As Paul wrote in 1 Corinthians chapter 13, true love always hopes, always perseveres.

* * * * * * *

Q: My boss, who is a lesbian, recently married her girlfriend. Now my husband and I have been invited to their wedding reception, and I don't know what to do. I don't agree with what they're doing or the lifestyle they are living, but she is my boss and I can't be rude. I also want to be a loving Christian. Any advice?

A: In the workplace, discrimination is illegal. And so the fact that you work with or do business with a gay person does not mean that you endorse his or her lifestyle. You are treating people with equality. If you are invited to your boss' gay wedding reception, your attendance there *does not constitute an endorsement of either the gay lifestyle or gay marriage.* In the same way, if you were going to the wedding of a straight couple who had been together immorally for five years, your attendance does not constitute an endorsement of the fact that they were living together without wedlock all that time. Your attendance at the birthday party of an alcoholic does not constitute an endorsement of her abusive drinking.

I would say that you don't want to destroy your relationships with people. There may come a time when you are able to share what God's Word says. But if you shun and boycott people, it will build a wall and they may never listen to you again. Your boss has probably not done any serious Bible study on homosexuality and perhaps does not even accept the Bible. Perhaps she is not aware that she is rebelling against God.

What would be the point of boycotting the wedding? To punish her? Place yourself on a higher moral plane and show you're above her? Change her?

God doesn't need you to punish anybody else. He will take care of the punishing. You and I aren't morally superior to anybody on earth—we are in as desperate need of Christ's forgiveness as anybody else. We are starving beggars who need God's food too. Change her? If you shun her, you will never be allowed into her mind and heart again.

In summary: go, and then watch for your opportunity for witness to Christ at an appropriate time.

4

"Do not conform to the pattern of this world, but be transformed by the renewing of your mind. Then you will be able to test and approve what God's will is—his good, pleasing and perfect will" (Romans 12:2).

Life Questions

Q: Can you give me some advice on how I can get my life more on God's agenda? I feel like I'm already so busy running my kids to sports practice, working full time, and then cooking the meals that I don't even have time for my own agenda.

A: I know how that happens. Without a lot of fanfare, as children join the household, you get locked into a frantic rush each day and never feel on top of things. You are constantly in reaction mode. If you don't intentionally think, "What am I truly needed for?" and if you are maybe a little insecure about yourself, you feel like you have to respond to everybody else's time needs in your daily agenda. Parental guilt is a terrible slave master. You can never do enough for others, and on top of it nobody seems particularly appreciative.

Here are some things to try:

1. Delegate. Maybe there could be more teamwork in the home. Review your workload and that of your spouse and see if there's balance. As children grow,

they can learn to do household chores. Insist on it and spend the time to show that you mean business with your expectations. Children can learn to do simple meal preparation, do dishes, clean, and help with the younger children.

2. Set some boundaries to what you can manage, and give yourself permission to say no. You are not a terrible parent if all your kids are not three-sport-a-year participants. Perhaps other parents can swing club sports for their kids in the off-season. You are not a loser parent if you say that you just can't do it.

3. Don't torment yourself with unsustainable expectations of what devotional Bible study looks like. You may not have 45 minutes of uninterrupted time each day. But you could set aside 5 minutes and guard that time, making it a regular habit. You can keep a prayer journal and write down the names of three people you're praying for each day.

4. You could use an audio Bible and listen to some Word while you're driving your commute. When you're hauling kids to their activities, see if you can get them to take their earbuds out and listen to some Christian music with you.

5. Realize that tending to your young children and to your spouse is God's agenda. Building a strong, love-filled home is the most important ministry you have right now. Embrace it! Soon, so soon, the kids won't need you anymore. Right now even your car trips are fabulous ways to communicate with them—you are all trapped in a small steel box and have to talk to each other.

• • • • • • •

Q: I want to be positive and happy, but every winter
the weather gets cold, the snow falls, it's dreary and dark
outside, and I just feel sad. Sometimes it makes me feel like
I'm weak in my faith. Do you have any advice?

A: I would encourage you to take this very seriously. Some
people call the malady SAD—Seasonal Affective Disorder—
and it affects a lot of people who live in the north and central
parts of the country. In fact, too many winter days without
sunshine and I can feel my own spirits dragging too. It's a
big deal.

There are things that you can do. First of all, anticipate it.
That season is going to come and there is a lot less light; the
farther north you live, the longer and darker the days. One
of the special joys of the Christmas season in the north is
that we binge on Christmas lights in our homes. My wife has
our house lit up like a night club from Thanksgiving to Ash
Wednesday—it helps us endure the long, dark nights. There
is a special coziness and warmth to this time. Have friends
over a lot.

I know what's helped some friends of mine with SAD is to
sit under a special sunlamp—they're called light boxes. They
substitute for sunlight, and in some people they trick the
brain into thinking that maybe it's still autumn. If you get
the type that emits UV rays, you might get the benefit of the
Vitamin D, whose winter deficiency many doctors think adds
to the SAD sad feelings. Or—maybe you can sneak in a little
getaway visit in January or February and go someplace south
and warm to break up the long winter. Talk to your doctor
about how you feel. I'm not a big fan of taking drugs for
every problem, but some people's chemical makeup leaves

them vulnerable to depression. The right medication can even out some people's emotional swings.

SAD has nothing to do with your faith—it is a physiological thing. Don't put yourself into a guilt trip. And hey—the upside of living in our latitudes is that we get extra daylight back in summer. Can't wait!

● ● ● ● ● ● ●

Q: What do I do with my doubts and "How can this be?" questions?

A: I think I know why you are so nervous about your lack of confidence in certain aspects of your faith. One of Jesus' disciples, Thomas, was nicknamed *Didymus* ("the Twin"). Because of his refusal to believe in Jesus' physical resurrection at first, insisting on touching Jesus' nail-printed hands, he got an even more permanent moniker: Doubting Thomas. If he was an identical twin, maybe he knew from personal experience how people could confuse identities and that gave him a suspicious and skeptical mind.

You have probably read James 1:6–8 on prayer: **"When you ask, you must believe and not doubt, because the one who doubts is like a wave of the sea, blown and tossed by the wind. That person should not expect to receive anything from the Lord. Such a person is double-minded and unstable in all they do."**

Ouch! Who among us, pastors and theological scholars included, has not struggled with understanding and accepting everything in Scripture? So many of God's most important promises are invisible to our eyes and often find their fulfillment in the future. We grow weary while we wait; our patience sometimes frays away.

Jesus doesn't despise you for your moments of shaky faith. He has great compassion for you in your times of struggle. He himself had to wrestle daily with Satan's temptations and felt the urge to doubt his Father's wisdom and love. He understood the stresses on his fearful and confused disciples: **"The spirit is willing, but the flesh is weak"** (Matthew 26:41). Neither does Jesus want those who are stronger in faith to look down on the strugglers: **"Be merciful to those who doubt"** (Jude 1:22).

Here is a strategy:

- *Don't struggle alone.* Talk to your family, fellow congregation members, your pastor. Explain why you have difficulty with a certain teaching or section of Scripture. Let others who have weathered your storm help you navigate.

- *Stay in the Word.* The Bible alone is our source of absolute truth and spiritual power. Everything that God needs us to know about him can be found there, and our understanding and comprehension and confidence grow slowly and steadily.

- *Pray.* Ask for clarity and confidence.

- *Don't panic.* As you read the stories of the great Bible heroes, you will notice that they all faltered at times. God actually builds our faith through testing, and he wants to build yours too, not tear you down. Don't give up! Peace will come.

●　●　●　●　●　●　●

Q: Is it bad that I love my life? Jesus said that whoever loves his life will lose it, but can't I love my life and keep it?

A: Of course you can love your life. Is it not full of God's blessings? Didn't he give you your life, family, friends, skills, and possessions to give you joy?

Read Jesus' words in their context: they come from John 12:25. Jesus was literally a matter of hours from his condemnation and crucifixion, and he knew it and was thinking about it constantly. He spoke on the powerful rhythm of God's rescue plan for the world—death, burial, and rebirth. He used a Jewish teaching device called a *mashal*—stating an extreme, even to the point of exaggeration, to make a point crystal clear for his listeners. He had done that same thing in the Sermon on the Mount, as when he talked about Christians gouging out an eye or cutting off a hand (see Matthew 5).

His point was not to create a mass of believers, all of whom went about depressed and hating their lives. His real point—that the believers come to regard Jesus Christ as their greatest treasure, their pearl, and be willing to suffer any loss, even life itself, rather than give up their relationship with their Savior.

That point was not just academic—in a short time terrible persecutions would erupt all over the Roman world. Believers would sometimes be forced to choose between Christ and their possessions, their freedom, and even their very lives. Many were martyred. Jesus' words give comfort to these and all Christian martyrs that even death cannot keep people from immortality in heaven. In fact, just as a kernel of wheat finds its true destiny by being planted in the ground and then erupting into new growth with hundreds more kernels, we Christians will not suffer by being planted in the ground. We will burst forth in reflected resurrection glory when he calls us.

• • • • • • •

Q: How do I find purpose at my older age when it seems as though I've already lived my life?

A: I've got to take issue with the way that question ends: "already lived my life." Oh man, you have not already lived your life! You have a unique value that you bring no matter which decade of your life you're in—in your 40s, 50s, 60s, 70s, 80s, even 90s or maybe you even broke 100. You're still working for God, and he is still proud to have you on his team.

As you get older, you are still valuable to God, though you may now have a different platform. Your voice is needed for different things. Let's just take your congregation, for instance—you're not heading up boards or committees any longer. But it becomes crucial that you help raise up a next generation of leaders, that you invest them with the authority and dignity they need. Not nitpicking, "Man, that's not how we used to do it," but to encourage and build them up so that there will be a transition and the organization will still flourish when you're gone.

It is a gift that you can give them—that you show your approval, that you clap and cheer for the people who are going to be replacing you. It is important that people who once were leaders learn to be regular workers again and do it gracefully without whining or complaining or without being miserable about how "this is different from the way we used to do it." You can choose to roll with the changes in a graceful way. The next generation will do things differently from yours, but some of their changes will be really good.

You can be the keeper and teller of the family stories. You can assemble your family's genealogy before the elders depart with all their knowledge. You can identify photographs of relatives whom only you remember. You now have much more disposable income and assets than the young folks and can make much larger gifts to your church's capital campaigns. You can do your legacy will and tax planning before age robs you of the clarity of your mind.

You can invest in the education of your grandkids so that they can compete in a knowledge economy. When you retire, you will finally have the time to volunteer for ministries and community projects that you were too busy for in your working years. You finally have time to set up a prayer schedule for key leaders in your world. You can help watch toddlers on Sunday so that frazzled moms and dads can actually get something out of a service for once.

If you are tempted to think that these things aren't much, just remember that the attitude most highly praised by Jesus is the humble attitude of a servant. We appreciate you! **"Stand up in the presence of the aged; show respect for the elderly and revere your God"** (Leviticus 19:32).

• • • • • • •

Q: I have cancer. How can I handle this trial and stay faithful through it?

A: We all dearly love the illusion that we will live trouble-free on this earth, that our lives will get better and better; we will accumulate wealth, possessions, friends, and fame; live healthy and active lives till we're 110; and then peacefully pass away in our sleep. It's other people who have the crises, right? Until you have your crisis.

Cancer is one of the most dreaded diseases because it works just like Satan—on the inside, sneaky, silent, and by the time you find out about its work it can be far along its deadly course.

Your illness can serve as a stage where you can have a powerful effect on your "audience"—friends, family, and caregivers. You can live the gospel confidence that you have been singing about in hymns all your life. You can call on God to keep his promise to display his working in your life (John 9:3). You can minister to people by letting them serve you. You can cheerfully submit to people doing things for you that you used to do for yourself, and yielding to those indignities with grace.

You can pray that God would stretch out your life to make sure that you have accomplished your mission on this earth (only he will know when it's done). You can vacuum up everything the Bible says about heaven. If your mobility is restricted, you will have time to do the praying you once wished you had time for. You can make a chart of people who need God's hand of blessing, and then pray through your cycle and release those blessings on them.

You can pray for healing and give your doctors every chance to use today's incredible scientific advances to keep you going. You can make a quiet, inner decision not to complain, not to let Satan warp your soul into being cynical and bitter. You can take inventory of your life's assets and choose to prize the gospel of Christ as your best and most beautiful possession. You can thank Jesus every day for Easter, for when disease finally has its way with your body, that will only accelerate your path to your own Easter and grand entrance into heaven.

● ● ● ● ● ● ●

Q: When you are tempted to do something you know is wrong, what helps you stand strong and not do it?

A: What a dilemma! As long as our lives last on this earth, we will be living in a state of war with Satan. He tests and tempts us every day, probing for weaknesses and vulnerabilities. What to do?

- Know that temptations will be coming and build yourself up in advance. Sin is just like cancer—once you've experienced it, it is never gone. You are never cured. Cancerous cells can always come back, and so does temptation even to a sin you thought you had "mastered." Be on guard and expect a counterattack.

- Fix your eyes on Jesus. Be aware of his presence at all times. Talk out loud to him when you feel the urges to rebel. Realize that he can see everything you're doing, and celebrate that his victory over Satan shows that his power is greater.

- Keep your feet from going into places that could get you into trouble. If you are an alcohol sinner, don't go into bars. If you have gambling fever, don't play even small-stakes bingo or play cards for nickels with your friends. If you are tempted to cheat on your wife, don't be alone with coworkers or friends who catch your eye.

- Have a touch with God's Word every day, even if only briefly. Let the stories of sinful rebellion and the disastrous consequences on those pages keep you aware of the high stakes.

- End each devotional moment with prayer. If Jesus needed to pray like crazy for strength against Satan, how could we not take advantage of its power even more?

- Let Jesus' wonderful gospel forgiveness for your past
  failures wash over you so that you don't feel that
  resistance is futile. His grace is new every morning.
  Washed in the blood of the Lamb, you can begin each
  day cleansed and pure and fight on. The gospel drives
  out depression and fear and gives you new incentive to
  put God first in all things.

* * * * * * *

Q: Can the devil read my mind or hear my thoughts?

A: Probably not. There is no passage of Scripture which
says that in so many words. Satan is not an evil version of
God. He is a creature himself, built as an angel, but whose
will and agenda have become totally warped. He is not
omnipresent like God. He is not omniscient (all-knowing)
nor omnipotent (all-powerful).

But having said those things, we still need to take the
threat he poses extremely seriously. Though he is not
omnipresent, he seduced a third of the angels to follow his
rebellion (Revelation 12:4), and thus he has a vast army of
helpers all over the world. His demons are able to invade and
take control of people and animals. On Maundy Thursday
evening, Satan himself entered into Judas as he dipped
his hand into the Passover dish (John 13:27). Satan filled
Ananias' heart (Acts 5:3). Ephesians 2:2 calls him the **"ruler
of the kingdom of the air, the spirit who is now at work in
those who are disobedient."**

The point of all this is that even if he can't read our
minds, he can read our behaviors. He has been studying
people for many thousands of years and knows how to
manipulate us. He and his demons can whisper ideas

at us in order to persuade us to rejoin and support his rebellion. **"The god of this age has blinded the minds of unbelievers, so that they cannot see the light of the gospel"** (2 Corinthians 4:4) and **"leads the whole world astray"** (Revelation 12:9).

Our own sinful nature is an ally of Satan and sympathetic to what he wants. We won't be rid of it until we get to heaven, and in the meantime we must keep it in subjection.

That's why the apostles urge us to recognize that we are in the midst of spiritual warfare, much more dangerous than the jungles of Vietnam or the desert around Fallujah, Iraq. Arming ourselves with prayer and study of Scripture is like putting God's helmet on our heads, so that the devil's blows won't confuse our thoughts, and putting a breastplate over our hearts and vital organs, so that Satan won't be able to manipulate our emotions with his lies (Ephesians 6:10-17).

In heaven we will be free of him forever. Come soon, Lord Jesus.

* * * * * * *

Q: What's the best way to let God fill me up when I feel like I'm empty? Sometimes talking to him feels like a one-way conversation.

A: I think I know what you mean. In a sense, praying is like talking to God on the phone but having to leave a message on his voicemail because we're not able to have a conversation in real time. That's kind of frustrating, isn't it? We want answers right away.

Personal closeness with God himself, the ability to interact directly, and the ability to perceive his presence by our five senses was something that the human race lost with

Adam and Eve's rebellion. They were expelled from Paradise. But Jesus has reversed those losses, and when we die we will reenter Paradise and enjoy God's presence directly.

In the meantime, know this: everything you say and pray to God is heard by him. Not a one of your messages to him falls to the ground. He hears everything you say; he cares about the content of what you are saying that you need; he answers, in his own way and in his time, every need that you present to him. Sometimes that answer is no; sometimes it's later, and sometimes he delivers immediately. We tend to be so ADD that we quickly forget our prayers of last month and don't even notice that God actually dealt with our problem. I don't know about you, but I know I don't thank him enough.

The other part of your question deals with your emotional needs. Obviously you won't get an immediate verbal response from God when you pray. But you can glean important wisdom on the way God operates by reading and hearing his Word. You will gain confidence in his wisdom, that he knows what he's doing. You will gain confidence in his power as you witness the unlimited power of the Sovereign of the universe. And your heart will grow in confidence of his rock-steady, unconditional, *personal* love for you and all believers.

Pay attention also to the wonderful people whom God sends into your life. You do not have to struggle alone. We all crave sudden and miraculous solutions, preferably dramatic and visible. God seems to prefer quiet and measured solutions, either by strengthening us to fix things ourselves or by working in our lives through other people. Either way he is showing that he cares about your needs.

Look backward into your life and remember the troubles that God helped you through. Let the grateful glow of a thankful heart fill you up and give you confidence that he will do it again.

* * * * * * *

Q: What does God say about what we read or watch on TV or at the movies that might have sinful actions in them?

A: You might also include in that list the theater plays we attend, the music we listen to, the books and poetry we read, and the online videos we consume.

It's pretty hard to interact with the world around us and hear and view the stories of its people without encountering sin. The world's greatest literature, dramas, music, and poetic sagas have plots that involve betrayal, envy, revenge, adultery, lying, stealing, pride, and murder. In fact the stories of the Bible are full of those very things. We need to be reminded of the all-pervasive nature of the sinful infection of humanity. We need to be reminded of God's judgment upon all evil, and we need to see that sin does not bring long-term satisfaction, happiness, or peace.

The danger, of course, is what we consume that might inflame *us* to sin like that. If you have violent tendencies, viewing violent movies might feed your violent imagination and lower your resistance to acting out like that. If you have money sickness, reading about unscrupulous Wall Street hustlers might give you ideas about how to take advantage of people.

The worst threat is the power of sexual stories and images. The sex industry has much to gain from encouraging men to see women as consumable resources, always willing, always available, always obedient. The sex industry has much to gain from encouraging women to use their formidable sexual powers to try to get men's attention, money, and love.

How do you know when you might be crossing God's line? Perhaps

- when you would be ashamed to have Jesus with you in the theater, watching your computer screen, or in your den watching the movie with you.

- when you would be ashamed to have your spouse or your parents watching with you.

- when it involves "enjoying" a sin that you have been told or are aware is a personal weakness.

Respect the corrupting power of your enemy. Always put God in the middle of your life. **"Whatever you do, do it all for the glory of God"** (1 Corinthians 10:31).

• • • • • • •

Q: Philanthropy is encouraged in our society, and that's a good thing. But good works won't get you to heaven, right?

A: Correct. **"It is by grace you have been saved, through faith—and this is not from yourselves, it is the gift of God—***not by works,* **so that no one can boast"** (Ephesians 2:8,9). People of means may make legacy gifts to their communities for a variety of reasons, some of which may be less than honorable, such as trying to "atone" for past crimes or to burnish their community standing or advance in social, business, or political circles.

But the basic meaning of *philanthropy* is that you love people. That term could also apply to you and your labors or gifts for your community, even if you are not wealthy. Rich people don't own the term. When you volunteer your time and energy to help people in need, build a community institution, tend the human machinery of community organizations like polling booths or blood drives or food pantries, you are a philanthropist.

But do those things because you love people, not to puff yourself up. Do them because you know it will please God. Do those things not in order to be saved but because you are grateful that you have already been saved by the blood of Jesus. Do them because all your possessions and money really belong to God anyway. He's just letting you use them.

• • • • • • •

Q: What about when you work for a boss who has no integrity, who seems to take pleasure in finding or making up faults, one who resents your Christian faith, and who overall is an abusive power-hungry micromanager who cannot even say good morning to you in a pleasant way? When do you know it is time to preserve some self-respect and leave the situation?

A: Find a better job.

But you know that already, and I suspect that if you had alternatives that were clearly superior, you'd have bailed already. Your real dilemma is how to cope on a day-to-day basis with a boss who is overly demanding, harsh, ungrateful, and dishonest. It may indeed mean the end of your employment there—you might get fired because you won't play his or her games, or you quit because you can't stand the working environment even before you've found another job.

My heart goes out to you right now. Know that Jesus never lets himself be out-given and that whatever you sacrifice for him in the short term will be repaid one hundred times over. St. Peter wrote to Christian servants and slaves who found themselves in unjust situations: **"In reverent fear of God submit yourselves to your masters, not only to those who are good and considerate, but also to those who are harsh"** (1 Peter 2:18). Anybody can hate a bad boss. It takes a Christian to stay sweet and kind, keeping your voice soft, avoiding backbiting and undermining, and just doing your job to the best of your ability.

I heard a story once of an employee who got chewed out publicly by a grouchy boss. "How could you stand it?" asked a fellow worker. He replied, "Oh, he has to live with himself all the time, and I just figured that I could stand it for five minutes."

Take your need to the Lord in prayer, and then keep your eyes open for another offer. It might be worth it to you to take less money for a job that brings a more pleasant work environment.

● ● ● ● ● ● ●

Q: What's the best way to let go and let God? Do you ever struggle with that?

A: You bet. I think the reason why we get frustrated is we are all kind of aggressive by nature; we want to take *control*. We want things *our* way; we want to manage and make things happen on *our* timetable to get what *we* want. But God doesn't always agree that our ways are the best ways.

God also really wants us to perceive and trust his interacting in our lives. Sometimes he allows us to hit a wall where we can't make it happen anymore. It's humbling to say, "I can't" (especially for the 50 percent of us in the world who are males). We *hate* admitting defeat. We hate asking for help. Why do you think we drive in circles for half an hour before we pull over and ask for directions?

Sometimes God has to let me hit a wall and wear out so that I say, "Lord, you need to do this. Lord, I am over my head. I need your help." And then he wants me to trust him that that prayer will get home to his throne in heaven. He wants me to trust that he's going to process it and take care of it at the right time. *His* right time.

Now, I don't always do that cheerfully and easily. I resonate with this question because I agree that letting go can be hard. But that's one of the benefits of aging. The older I get, the more cheerfully I am willing to yield when I can't control a situation. In my youth, I had much greater strength and energy than I do now, but also a load of impatience. But these days, along with the diminishing of energy with age comes *a serenity* as I watch God at work.

And here, I guess, would be my best answer of all to this dilemma—look backward at your life. Look at the ways in which everything fits together. Everything in your past has been woven together and is blessed by the Lord. As I consider my own life, so many things that I wanted didn't happen. But so many things I *never* would have dreamed of *did* happen—not because of my actions, but because of *God's* arranging things and pulling things together.

My life has taken so many unusual twists and turns because *God* was guiding and steering. At the time I probably was pretty frustrated. I need to do what I can when there is a problem or challenge within my ability. But when I run out of gas, when I hit a wall, when something stops, when something isn't happening that I wanted, it's great to sit down by the side of the road, maybe find a little park bench, and take a couple of deep breaths. I make sure I'm not driving the people around me crazy and say "I love you" about 15 or 20 times to the amazing people in my life.

I'll take another deep breath and say to the Lord, "I don't understand what's happening now. It isn't what I would have chosen. But if something I wanted isn't happening, it must mean that *you* are now stepping in and your guiding hands are at work. And since, Lord, I can completely trust your Fatherly heart, I can completely trust your brilliance and wisdom; and since there is no limit to your power, I'm going to sit on this bench for a while and watch and see what you're going to do. Now, Lord, my prayer is for you to stimulate and improve my hearing and my vision so that I can perceive what you're up to. When you're ready for me to get off the bench and start moving again, I'll be ready for your agenda and your plan."

Want to sit on my park bench with me for a little bit?

• • • • • • •

Q: What's the best way to make Jesus the center of your life all the time, not just on Sundays?

A: I'm a very visual person, so you know what works for me? Christian art. I love finding beautiful representations of our Savior and his life and work and putting them in strategic places around our home, church, and school. I love the feeling of having his eyes on me, and I also love the feeling of keeping my eyes on Jesus. I love artwork involving the cross—it reminds me of the terrible expense of the purchase of my salvation, but it reminds me also how valuable I must be to Jesus.

When I want to focus my attention on a life change that I

want to make, I put Post-it notes next to my computer screen or on the fridge door at eye level. When I want to keep my thoughts God-centered during the day, I pop a Christian music CD in the player, pull up sacred music on my computer, or tune in a Christian station on my car radio and sing along if I know the words.

Get involved in a choir or in a weekday small Bible study group. The other people will provide insights you wouldn't have thought of yourself, and they will illustrate Scripture's teachings with stories from their lives that make the doctrines come alive.

Probably nothing beats a careful, planned, intentional, regular time that you set aside for good old Bible reading. It doesn't have to be a lengthy study. It is more important that it be regular, at a predictable time, and that you slowly work your way through all the books of the Bible. And then do it again. Take notes right in the Bible as you figure things out. Underline and highlight and add arrows and asterisks. That way the next time you read that portion, you won't be puzzled by things you had once figured out. Always read from the same book, so that you get familiar with the page layout. It will help you find things more quickly.

● ● ● ● ● ● ● ●

Q: I know I'm supposed to trust God for my daily bread, but does that mean it's a sin to stockpile if I find a good deal?

A: Goodness, no.

There can be multiple causes as to why things happen. If a farmer has a great harvest loaded into his barns and bins in November, was it because he worked hard or because God blessed his fields? The answer is yes. They are both true. If a student graduates from college with honors, was it because the student worked so hard or because God gifted her with persistence, ambition, and a bright mind? The answer is yes.

Back in the day, when life insurance was a new thing, some Christians made it an issue of conscience not to buy it. They thought it showed a lack of trust in God, or that it was gambling with their lives because it made them more valuable dead than alive. Nonsense. Protecting your family by investing in a risk pool is nothing but good planning. The same thing happened when social security began—so many pastors were so adamant about this supposed "lack of trust in God" that many were allowed to opt out of it.

It's important that we don't pit two good ideas against each other. Is it important to trust God for daily bread? Absolutely. Is it important to know that God has made certain promises that his children will always eat and have shelter? Yes. Does that mean that therefore it's sinful if you try to accumulate wealth or that you build up your food supplies or that you would have a disciplined savings plan in anticipation of a day when you want to retire and stop working your day-to-day job? You can stockpile too much, of course. Some people have such anxiety about scarcity that they become hoarders. But it is not Christian common sense to pit trust and hard work and planning against each other. They are all good things.

The Scriptures encourage us to be thrifty, to save, to accumulate wealth for our families so we can support the people we love and to enable us to be generous in our communities and to ministries that we care about. I'd encourage you to do both things: trust God every day for what you need but also have a plan to build up your family's resources in anticipation of when you will have to retire, and also so that you personally can be a generous giver.

● ● ● ● ● ● ●

Q: I've been without a job for several months now. I am without money for bills. Emotionally, I have been very depressed. How can I feel God's touch and see his plans for me?

A: Your life situation right now really hurts my heart to hear. Sadly it is part of the human experience ever since the fall into sin for people to be terribly squeezed for resources at times.

You have already partly answered your own question by going to the Lord in prayer. God wants to hear from us, and he allows us often in our lives to come under pressure so that he hears from us. And I can tell you in my own life the times when I've prayed the least is when I don't feel I need any help. The times when I've been most dialed into God's Word and prayer is when I have felt isolated or under pressure and running on fumes. **"This poor man called, and the Lord heard him; he saved him out of all his troubles. The angel of the Lord encamps around those who fear him, and he delivers them"** (Psalm 34:6,7).

Look back in your life. You've been stressed for several months, but look back farther. Remember all the resources that God sent earlier in your life when things were smoother. He does care about you! The Father who made things happen for you once will do it again in his time.

Also—note from Scripture that God doesn't usually perform dramatic and visible miracles when his people are in need. He prefers to send quiet resources, people resources, all around us. When we go through these times, he just doesn't send a magic parachute, an airdrop with bundles of used twenties neatly tied together; he sends us people. People helping people is God's usual rescue plan, I think. And don't forget your church. Talk to your pastor. Sometimes he's got ideas that can help network you to the help and strength and resources that you will need.

● ● ● ● ● ● ●

Q: I see so-called psychics on TV all the time. Where do they get their powers to predict the future? Is it from God?

A: They aren't predicting the future. They are pretending to predict the future to get attention and money.

If you want a good laugh, buy a copy of one of the supermarket tabloids in December and clip out the articles from the psychics who think they can predict what will be happening in the year to come. Put the article in a drawer and pull it out a year later. Showbiz "psychics" read newspapers and watch TV and know what people are anxious about. They make educated guesses about the future, and get a few right, which they then trumpet loudly. You never hear them apologize for the 90 percent they got wrong.

Only God knows the future. Even Satan has to go day by day.

There is such a powerful market for secret information and insider knowledge of the future that people have been posing as psychics for millennia. Every royal court in the ancient world had its soothsayers, mystics, prophets, astrologers, and mediums. The Bible warns us to stay away from them—they are all knowing or unknowing agents of Satan: **"When someone tells you to consult mediums and spiritists, who whisper and mutter, should not a people** inquire of their God? Why consult the dead on behalf of the living? *Consult God's instruction* and the testimony of warning. If anyone does not speak according to this word, they have no light" (Isaiah 8:19,20).

The more you know your Bible, the less you will be tempted by TV psychics.

● ● ● ● ● ● ●

Q: Does Baptism really save or is it just symbolic?

A: Your question lies at the fault line between two major segments of Christendom. It's a big deal. At stake is the very nature of Baptism itself, how we relate to God, power and authority within the church, and our confidence of being God's people.

First of all, let's be clear. Jesus Christ alone is our Savior and the source of our salvation. He alone is the Way, the Truth, and the Life. He alone is the **"pioneer and perfecter of faith"** (Hebrews 12:2). It was his obedience that now becomes our own; it was his body that took the blows, his blood that was shed for our forgiveness, his burial tomb that enclosed his lifeless body, and his resurrection that makes ours possible. His work was given to all mankind of all ages—this is called God's unconditional *grace.*

To be saved from your sins, however, it is necessary to believe in Christ. **"It is by grace you have been saved,** *through faith"* (Ephesians 2:8). We cannot generate our own faith—it must be given to us by the Holy Spirit through the power of the Word of God. Faith connects individual sinners with the forgiving grace of Christ.

Baptism's power does not come from the faith of the individual who performs it. It does not inhere in the water.

The water is ordinary and can do nothing in and of itself. The "saving" happens when a human being speaks God's words and applies the water to the individual (the manner of the application is left by Scripture to our discretion). Baptism is nothing less than a **"washing of rebirth and renewal of the Holy Spirit"** (Titus 3:5). Because the water of Baptism is supercharged with the Word of God that is being spoken, it is a watery way of applying God's Word directly to an individual.

The individual receiving Baptism doesn't do anything to affect the power of the baptism. He or she is just the receiver, as when a child receives a bequest or legacy from a relative who passed away. Baptism's blessings are God's gifts, not wages or the fruits of our work. All that remains to us is to appreciate our new status, for **"all of you who were baptized into Christ have clothed yourselves with Christ"** (Galatians 3:27).

In a sense, then, it is appropriate for St. Peter to say that Baptism saves us: **"This water** (i.e., of the great flood) **symbolizes baptism** *that now saves you* **also—not the removal of dirt from the body but the pledge of a clear conscience toward God"** (1 Peter 3:21). It is nothing less than one of the means by which sinners like you and me are connected to Christ.

● ● ● ● ● ● ●

Q: I just listened to your sermon series *Money or Mammon*. In it you cite from Proverbs that God wants to abundantly bless us, to "spoil us rotten," and gives us as much as we can handle. How do we know that those passages in Proverbs are speaking of physical material blessings now and not just a richer faith toward God as we display our faith in him or the blessing of heaven in the future?

If God wants to bless us as much as we can handle, what can we say to the person who is doing as you say that God desires for us (i.e., trying to advance his or her career while trying to serve God, learn about God, and invest properly to gain more wealth), but it has not happened for them?

Finally, are there other spots in the Bible where God says he wants to abundantly bless us *now* with health, wealth, and prosperity, along with the future heaven that Jesus paid for? Please balance that with going through trials, i.e., financial trouble, health/family issues, etc.

A: 1) Sometimes poverty in the Bible does indeed mean spiritual poverty, but usually it is then so identified. When simple statements are made about money, let's not overthink and overinterpret. The best Bible interpretation is usually the simplest understanding of the plain words. When Jesus wanted to make a point about spiritual poverty (i.e., people who knew that they were morally bankrupt), he said things like, "Blessed are the poor *in spirit*." When Proverbs talks about prosperity, the simplest and plainest way to understand those words is material prosperity.

Making money, having money, spending money, and saving money are not evil in and of themselves. Wealth goes sour only when we become addicted to it, selfish with it, and forget to give glory to the Giver of it.

2) Only God knows what role he desires us to fill on this earth. Everybody I know has been spoiled rotten with far more than he or she needs. Even the poorest person in America enjoys many luxuries that King Solomon himself could never have dreamed of, including the palaces of education that our schools are today compared with those of older eras, the staggering miracles of health care available to

all, and the miraculous speeds at which we now can travel.

Some people are blessed with working-class and middle-class lives. Some have to suffer financial and health setbacks and have a platform to glorify God in that way. Others have been gifted with a staggering load of material wealth and now have the burden of managing a load of funds, investing well, and disbursing large amounts of charitable donations without making the recipients greedy or lazy.

3) Disasters do happen. People who try to invest carefully can get burned by bad investment advice. People who try to live healthy lifestyles tear hamstrings and crack vertebrae. People who live careful lives suffer car accidents caused by the negligence of others. In all of our life situations, God is in control, will limit the stress we are put under, will provide resources and healing, and will give us abundant opportunities to witness to our faith.

God sees and knows our sorrows, reverses, and especially the sacrifices we make for him. He keeps good notes and remembers. He does indeed sometimes pour special material blessings into our lives, not just in heaven someday but in the here and now. St. Peter once said to Jesus, **"'We have left everything to follow you!' . . . Jesus replied, 'No one who has left home or brothers or sisters or mother or father or children or fields for me and the gospel will fail to receive a hundred times as much *in this present age . . .* and in the age to come eternal life'"** (Mark 10:28-30).

●　●　●　●　●　●　●

Q: Do you think it's wrong for me to put my mom in a nursing home? She needs care, but I feel guilty about doing it and not taking care of her myself.

A: There are no right or wrong answers to this question. It's a life dilemma that many people have to go through. I've gone through it myself with tough decisions about caring for my frail and elderly father, and I'm sure I will have to again. What's at stake is what you owe the seniors in your life. Do you need to quit your job in order to provide in-home care? That's not a divine commandment; that's not something you are *required* to do. Some people choose to do it, and they deserve immense respect and compassion. Some people just can't financially—they need the income of their job. Some just can't physically move an elderly person around to the bed, bathroom, and shower.

The stress of these decisions also has a way of causing quarrels among the siblings. If you have to share this decision with others, almost inevitably one in the group will be quicker to urge moving a frail parent to assisted living and at least one will scramble for every last option to avoid institutional living. In addition, the sibling who lives geographically closest to the parent feels the extra burden of being the "go-to" caregiver.

So what to do? I guess my general advice for your dilemma is first of all to try to keep your parents in their home as long as possible. Familiarize yourself with all of the services that are around to enable people to put off living in an institution. But when the day comes that it's no longer possible to provide care, when your loved one is going to be a risk or danger to himself or herself, when they need a level of care *that you cannot provide*, make the hard decision without fear or shame or guilt. Help them adjust to this new stage in their lives.

P.S. When it becomes that stage in your own life, have your mind arranged in advance so that you can make that transition cheerfully.

● ● ● ● ● ● ●

Q: If my sister and her girlfriend, who say they are Christian, never leave the gay lifestyle, will I see them in heaven? It makes me sad to think about it.

—and—

Q: My brother is gay and lives with his boyfriend. Most of my family has shunned them. How do I show both of them God's love while communicating that I don't think their lifestyle is pleasing to God?

A: Any Christian who dares to utter an opinion on the sexuality of others better know what the Bible says. Do you know where the Scripture speaks about homosexuality? If our words are not based squarely on Scripture, then we will just appear driven by prejudice rather than principle.

Have you done your biblical homework? Read Romans chapter 1 three times slowly and carefully. Do the same with Matthew chapter 19 and with 1 Corinthians chapter 6. Any conversation you have with your sister or brother should not appear to be based on *your* opinions, tastes, or personal philosophy. You are merely God's flesh-and-blood messenger in their lives.

Key to this discussion is whether your family member and partner accept the authority of the Bible, or only some of it, or none of it. Sad to say there are Christian denominations and congregations representing all three of those points of view. Your sister or brother may find toleration and encouragement for the lifestyle from the leadership of the church he or she attends. If your brother or sister does not share a high view of Scripture with you, most of your discussions about human sexuality will be pointless.

It's important that you keep showing unconditional love for him or her. *That doesn't mean that you condone the lifestyle.* It just means that shunning and shaming will never change their hearts. Only the gospel, only love, can inspire people to change their hearts and behaviors.

My greatest regret about our country's recent legitimization of gay marriage is that it will damage the individuals themselves. Gay desires will always be there, but it is repentance that brings Christ's forgiveness and new strength. First Corinthians 6:9-11 teaches us that *arsenokoitai* (men who have sex with other men) will not inherit the kingdom of God. Romans 1:26 shows that women living the gay lifestyle fall under the same condemnation. Steadfast rejection of God's Word only brings divine judgment and condemnation.

We need to speak about this issue with great humility. God will make all the decisions on judgment day—and he will be right about everybody. Living a gay lifestyle is adultery, but it is important that we do not single out this particular type of adultery as any worse than straight people committing adultery. On a numerical basis, there are far more straight people than gay who are committing adultery, and those sins put them just as much at risk before God. What matters is repentance and claiming the blood-bought forgiveness of Jesus Christ and realigning our life decisions to get back in line with God's intent.

I would be very hesitant to make any pronouncements about where anyone is going to end up in eternity. What I would prefer to do is simply pass on God's message—simply, lovingly, and with an open heart that will submit to their critiques of the integrity of my lifestyle. What matters is not our personal view. What matters is that as Bible-believing

Christians we simply pass on what has been first given to us. We will let God sort out what happens to people in eternity.

It may be that some people who are right now living in some type of adultery still have faith in their hearts, a faith that's at war with their lifestyle. It's a mess and it's unresolved. For that matter, look at your own life and see some of the moral messes you are in right now where you haven't lived out the full implications of your faith. Let's just lay out God's Word, lay out his warnings, but lay out the wonderful promise from 1 Corinthians chapter 6 that says it is possible to make changes from an immoral lifestyle and come back to be with the Lord Jesus, come back and be washed and cleansed by his blood.

● ● ● ● ● ● ●

Q: I want you to tell me why God allowed his little children to be abused by priests. My son, at age 10, was abused for years. He was a mass server. Where in the Bible is an answer? He suffers with shame and memories.

A: My heart just hurts for you—to think that your child was abused by a person who should have been the safest and most secure protector must be just devastating. I don't blame you for crying out to God in pain and frustration—could he not have protected your son and kept him away from a pedophile?

There are no clear answers, for much of what goes on in the world is outside our ability to perceive and understand. Here are some things I've learned from the Bible and from life:

The human race chose to rebel against God, assuming that there would be no consequences. Adam and Eve and we are wrong—when our first parents invited evil into Paradise, they unleashed a tidal wave of misery upon themselves and their descendants. How do you suppose Mother Eve felt when she came upon the dead body of her son Abel (Genesis 4)? Do you think she didn't regret her foolish decision a million times? We are born sinful and thus are part of Adam and Eve's conspiracy to rebel against God. We are still experiencing the terrible consequences of thinking that Satan and his ways are good for us. They are not. His ways bring suffering and pain and death.

God thought us worth saving. He sent his Son, Jesus, to live completely in our world, as one of us, experiencing everything we experience, including rejection and suffering and death. God chose to pronounce forgiveness of sins on the whole world, and those who believe it have it. Jesus knows how your son feels. Jesus knows how you feel, for he completely lived our lives as our substitute. He loves you and has compassion for you and feels your pain. You have a Friend in heaven.

The Bible has many more stories of one human being abusing another. It even has stories of corrupt and rotten religious leaders who misuse their position for personal gain or pleasure (see 1 Samuel 2:12-22). God will hold such people accountable for their evil deeds—they will not slip through his net, and he will deal with each one appropriately.

Every catastrophe in life provides an equal opportunity. You and your son can decide to forgive his oppressor and in this way act just like Christ himself. Just as Christ forgives us our many sins and still loves us, we can show that same mercy to the fools and sinners and even criminals around us and let it go. We can open ourselves up to the healing of the gospel and let go of revenge fantasies, the endless prison of anger, or the continuing self-abuse of depression and self-hatred. I heard a wonderful and inspirational address a few months ago from a woman with no feet. She used the challenge to learn to walk, then run, then sprint on artificial feet. She used her disability to become a phenomenal track star. My counsel to you is to let God use your brokenness and pain and turn it inside out into strength. In this way you and your son can be God's agents of healing to other hurting people.

● ● ● ● ● ● ●

Q: What are some ways I can better control my temper?

A: You are wise to recognize the danger and the damage that a harsh tongue and intense emotions can cause. God thinks so too: **"Everyone should be quick to listen, slow to speak and slow to become angry, because human anger does not produce the righteousness that God desires"** (James 1:19,20). No kidding. Words spoken in anger can never be sucked back down the throat. Hurts given to others, especially in your family, will last years or even decades and will not go away even if you later say you're sorry. A lack of brakes on an angry mouth can lead to physical violence too.

Have a little sit-down with yourself and have a little self-reflective conversation. Ask yourself why your anger flashes up so quickly. Are you really insecure? Do you protect your weakness by going on the attack? Do you like yourself, or do you lash out at others because you don't like yourself very much? Do you have issues with trying to control everything, and maybe everybody, around you? Do you feel respected, or do you have to come on super strong to look tough? Did you grow up with a lot of shouting and anger in your home? Do you and your dad have a good relationship? Is your judgment in a spirited discussion maybe not as infallible as you would like to think?

Pick somebody close to you to be your anger monitor. Decide in advance to trust that person if he or she signals to you that you're losing it. The minute you catch yourself raising your voice or saying something punitive, stop it right there and apologize. And when you apologize, don't offer rationalizations of why you're so upset. That spoils everything. Just say how sorry you are and stop! Ask for forgiveness so that the healing can begin right away.

Keep a journal near your Bible and keep track for a month how many times a day you lose your temper. Celebrate your victories over Satan's temptations. Bask in the glow of being a forgiven, loved, and immortal child of God. Look for ways to repair damage you've done by past outbursts. And finally, ask Jesus to instill in you the same patience that he showed in his Passion. You are not destined to stay in your same ruts. With God's help you can learn to listen better and speak more softly. It's worth the effort!

• • • • • • •

Q: What's a good way to respond when someone criticizes you?

A: Man, I wish I were better at that myself. My skin is way too thin sometimes, and I either want to shun and avoid the person or strike back and cut him even more deeply than he cut me.

Proverbs has a lot of wisdom to share with believers about how to deal with stress in our relationships, such as:

• **"Fools show their annoyance at once, but the prudent**

overlook an insult" (12:16). You don't have to respond to every dig. Just let some go whizzing past you and pretend you didn't hear them. It's possible the other person didn't mean to slam you as hard as you felt. If you let it go, you stop a war.

· **"The prudent keep their knowledge to themselves, but a fool's heart blurts out folly"** (12:23). If you retaliate, there's no stopping the escalation. Satan will tempt you to remember every glaring weakness of the other person right at that moment.

· **Where there is strife, there is pride, but wisdom is found in those who take advice"** (13:10). Listen to the criticism. After you get over your wounded feelings and wounded pride, you might detect that your critic has a point and there's something in your life that needs fixing.

· **"A gentle answer turns away wrath, but a harsh word stirs up anger"** (15:1). Anyone can lash back. It takes a Christian to feel the sting, take a deep breath, and answer gently. Assume the best and kindest possible explanations for other people's behavior—"She's having a bad day." "His home life is terrible." "She just got dumped by her boyfriend." "He's exhausted."

Even when you're hurt and angry about what's been said, you will always keep the door open if you end the conversation with, "I will think about what you said."

● ● ● ● ● ● ●

Q: I know it's wrong to lie, but what about a lie for the better good? (Your friend bought a new outfit and she asks you how it looks. Should you tell her it looks awful or say, "Oh, it looks great!" to preserve her feelings?)

A: You do well to state the basic principle first before looking around for exceptions. God thinks the truth so important that he forbade bearing false witness in the Ten Commandments. Paul wrote, **"Each of you must put off falsehood and speak truthfully to your neighbor"** (Ephesians 4:25). Lying is Satan's native language; Jesus called him a liar and the father of lies.

Children get good at it without any special training. You don't have to send them to summer lying camp or have remedial lying teachers to help them catch up. Lies are cheap ways to evade responsibility and gain advantage over other people.

Having said that, I think we could all honestly admit that being kind and courteous to one another may involve saying some things that aren't actually true, but we might wish them to be true. "Oh, that's okay. It's no bother." Actually, yes it was a bother and you're glad the chore is over. "I don't mind." Yes, you do mind, but you are sucking it up to give a gift of your labor to a friend. "I love my birthday present." Actually you don't love your birthday present, but you love the love behind it. See my point?

Now to your example. All of us face moments each day when people come to us looking for affirmation and approval. Don't reach too quickly for the escape of a cheap lie. What to do? Here are a few thoughts. First, beauty and appearance do not have absolute standards. They are relative and subjective, meaning that your affection for the person makes him or her look good no matter what. A husband who is committed to loving his wife till death us do part will always think her as beautiful as the day he married her.

Second, you can reframe the question. Ask about where the clothes came from. Show interest. Ask where it will be worn. Find some aspect to compliment. "I love that fabric!" Gush over a different outfit that she owns and maybe she'll get the hint that the other outfit looks better on her. Third, if you are a husband, always reward your wife for telling you the truth, no matter how blunt, about your appearance. She probably knows four times as much as you do about fashion and may spare you some serious embarrassment.

● ● ● ● ● ● ●

Q: How do I teach my kids to give joyfully?

A: Let them watch you making out your checks and preparing your own contributions. Let them listen to you talk about how important this is, the great things that your charitable gifts make happen, and the joy it gives you to be generous. Let them hear your words of faith that you know God will keep his great gifts coming. Let them know that you really believe that **"you will be enriched in every way so that you can be generous on every occasion, and through us your generosity will result in thanksgiving to God"** (2 Corinthians 9:11).

When you're in church, let them put the family offering in the basket and make it their act of worship as well. When there is a special project at church, ask them to contribute (even though their funds may be meager). In that way they will have buy-in to the project and will feel some "ownership" whenever they see or hear of it.

When their first income comes, from snow shoveling, chores, babysitting, or whatever, sit down with them and very slowly explain how to be intentional with income. I used to do that with all four of my kids. Ten percent would go back to God, ten percent went into their pocket as mad money, and eighty percent went into their college fund. I showed them how to keep a ledger.

Model for them that generosity is not just about giving money but giving of your time, of yourself. When you decide to volunteer for things, angle for things you can take the kids to and show them the joy of giving your service. Do things *with* them—serving in a food line, ushering, washing cars, helping a food pantry, recycling clothes and household items.

* * * * * * *

Q: My husband is a spender and I'm a saver. It causes a lot of arguments! Any advice for us?

A: You are wise to have calmly figured that out and articulated it so bluntly. It will help. I have three pieces of advice: pick your hills to die on, negotiate, and bend.

Identify for yourself the money principles and strategies that you absolutely must have. Perhaps it's an untouchable, rock-steady contribution to a 401(k) or other kind of tax-deferred annuity. Perhaps it's really strong life insurance coverage. Perhaps it's a nonnegotiable percentage of your income that you sock away. Which are your hills to die on?

Then enter the negotiations. Realize that you aren't going to get everything you might want. Explain your points of view clearly. Show why they make so much sense. But also listen, really listen, to what your husband is trying to tell you. Since some of the income comes from his labor, he gets a big say in the family's decisions. Help him isolate *his* nonnegotiable hills to die on and see if you can live with them. Agree on the maximum amount that each of you can spend without consulting the other. Take notes on things you can agree on as strategies so that there won't be confusion or arguments later, and keep it handy for reference.

Finally, decide for yourself on the areas where you can bend and yield gracefully. Explain to your husband the areas where you will insist, and be gracious when *he* lets you win on those points. Over time, as your financial security grows because of your planning and willpower, review your documents with him (without gloating) and show how a disciplined savings plan can seriously build the family's financial assets.

You know, there is something to love in both savers and spenders. Savers think long term (good!). Savers excel at self-denial (good!). Savers build up rainy-day funds so that they can withstand some financial reverses (good!). But savers can also become misers (bad!), cheapskates (bad!), and scroungers off others (bad!). Perhaps you can figure out what are the best features of your husband's more spendy ways and make them part of your family style: generosity to others, a willing giver at your church, instigator of spontaneous crazy fun that makes memories, and a cheerful trust in God that he will continue to bless you in the future: **"A generous person will prosper; whoever refreshes others will be refreshed"** (Proverbs 11:25).

●　●　●　●　●　●　●

Q: I know God says we need to tithe 10 percent, but my church is always encouraging me to give more and step up "beyond tithing." What do I do?

A: In our New Testament era, there are no sacred

commandments about the percentage of your income that you must give back to the Lord. Mandatory tithing belongs to the Old Covenant. Just as there are no mandatory annual religious festivals in the Christian era, no kosher dietary rules, and no hereditary priesthood, so there are no divine regulations about giving. In this era God chooses to view you as spiritual adults. You wouldn't tell your 35-year-old daughter what to give; God doesn't tell you either. He simply sends income your way, invites you to love and worship him back, and then trusts you to choose wisely.

Your gifts are your choice: **"Each of you should give what you have decided in your heart to give, not reluctantly or under compulsion, for God loves a cheerful giver"** (2 Corinthians 9:7). The primary drivers for all Christian giving is our relationship with our God, our gratitude for grace, our appreciation for his financial resources sent our way, and a desire to invest in ministry.

Our giving is not driven primarily by institutional needs. Churches should be careful about how they phrase their appeals to their members. Budgets, utility bills, capital campaigns, and operating deficits are all important issues, but they must never take the place of Christ at the center of our generosity thinking.

I know how easy it is for church leadership to sound a little desperate and use pressure tactics to stimulate giving. We might be struggling mightily to balance our books and pay off debts. We might have a tremendous burn to expand our facilities or programs. But we must never steal people's joy in giving; we must never replace the gospel's sweet pull with the push of pressure; we must never look like an insatiable money machine where what our members do is never enough.

Give what you have decided to give. Ask God to bless it. And then sleep well.

• • • • • • •

Q: I've heard you say that I can't outgive God. I feel like I'm giving generously and from the heart, but our family still struggles financially. What are we doing wrong?

A: You aren't doing anything wrong. If you are a generous giver and it comes from the heart, stop right there and feel really, really good about your relationship with God. He has healed you of the sin of stinginess; he has awakened in you a generous spirit; his precious gospel is at the center of your life. Enjoy every one of your gifts to the Lord; give them all freely as acts of sincere worship, and pray that God will bless your congregation's use of that money for inspirational ministry in your community and around the world.

God's Word promises that over time he will replace those gifts in your treasury and more: **"Remember this: whoever sows sparingly will also reap sparingly, and whoever sows generously will also reap generously. . . . God is able to bless you abundantly, so that in** *all* **things at** *all* **times, having** *all* **that you need, you will** *abound* **in every good work"** (2 Corinthians 9:6,8).

I had to laugh the other day when I came across financial records from my younger years. There was a stretch of *11 years* when my net worth stayed totally flat. I had hardly any financial cushion. In time God lifted me up, and he will do that for you and your family too. He just doesn't tell us when. God had reasons for keeping me financially humble in those years, and he wouldn't allow you to struggle right now unless he had a plan to make these situations work for your good in some way. Hang on! Soon comes relief.

• • • • • • •

Q: My husband just died of cancer, and his treatment and funeral have nearly bankrupted me. Now I'm alone *and* broke. Is this God's plan for me?

A: We are all dying to know if the things that happen to us, especially the bad things, were *sent* by God or just *allowed to happen* by him. This side of heaven we won't ever know, and that includes your situation. What we can say for sure is that God is okay with what happened because he has good plans for you, plans to bless you and not to harm you. Your life in the short term will be hard. You are experiencing personally what Paul told the believers in the Galatian cities: **"We must go through many hardships to enter the kingdom of God"** (Acts 14:22). But don't panic—**"Believers in humble circumstances ought to take pride in their high position** [in God's eyes]**"** (James 1:9). God in time will lift you up.

What to do in the meantime?

1. Don't be too proud to accept *and ask* for help. When people ask you what they can do for you, pause and think a minute and then tell them the truth about what you need right then and there. Don't say "I'm fine" if you don't mean it. That is neither whining nor complaining. God *designed* us to be interdependent; the Bible says that it is not good that the man should be alone, but it isn't so hot for the widow to be alone either. It may be that your need is God's gift to someone else with plenty who needs to exercise generosity at this time.

2. Do you have a financial advisor? If you don't, get one. Have him or her help you to minimize your taxes,

access social safety-net resources, and use your own slender resources wisely.

3. Let your pastor know about your situation. In many ways we pastors are resource crossroads—we help people make connections and serve one another. **"Religion that God our Father accepts as pure and faultless is this: to look after orphans and widows in their distress"** (James 1:27). You don't have to suffer in silence. You can't expect people to read your mind or know your financial situation by somehow reading your face.

4. You can let your extended family know your situation. Christians **"who [do] not provide for their relatives, and especially for their own household, have denied the faith and [are] worse than an unbeliever"** (1 Timothy 5:8).

* * * * * * *

Q: We're told to have 401ks and save for retirement. Does that mean we're "storing away in barns"?

A: You are referring, of course, to Jesus' famous parable about a rich fool. **"'Watch out! Be on your guard against all kinds of greed; life does not consist in an abundance of possessions.' And he told them this parable: 'The ground of a certain rich man yielded an abundant harvest. He thought to himself, "What shall I do? I have no place to store my crops." Then he said, "This is what I'll do. I will tear down my barns and build bigger ones, and there I will store my surplus grain. And I'll say to myself, 'You have plenty of grain laid up for many years. Take life easy; eat,** drink and be merry.'" But God said to him, "You fool! This very night your life will be demanded from you. Then who will get what you have prepared for yourself?" This is how it will be with whoever stores up things for themselves but is not rich toward God'" (Luke 12:15–21).

Here's what makes that man a fool—not that he was rich, but that everything was oriented around himself. Get a pencil and circle the words *I*, *my*, and *myself* in the reading above. It was not the storing of a great quantity of food that was the problem but rather storing it up *for himself*. He had money sickness. He had forgotten that he was merely a steward of God's treasures, or maybe he never knew it in the first place.

Throughout his earthly ministry Jesus depended for support on a vast network of friends who raised and prepared the food he ate and had bought the homes in which he slept. He was happy to benefit from the resources other people had saved up. His Father chose for him a life of poverty and humility, but that is not a universal expectation for all believers.

Scripture helps us develop a healthy attitude toward money—grateful for God's providing, happy to be working for his enterprises, willing to serve under his agenda, generous in church and community, thankful as employees who work hard and employers who are honest and fair. I hope that you not only use your company's 401(k) but that you don't leave money on the table and that you can make the full contribution to be matched.

● ● ● ● ● ● ●

Q: Is it wrong to want to make lots of money and live comfortably?

A: No. Christians don't have to aspire to a life of poverty and pain, although both misfortunes come upon believers and unbelievers alike. The fact that the Bible speaks a great deal about overcoming those hardships doesn't mean that they should be *life goals* for us.

Jesus did indeed tell the rich young ruler (Luke 18:18-30) to divest himself of all his assets and give them away. But that was specific advice for a specific situation. It is not a general command or principle for all believers of all time. That young man was addicted to his possessions—they had become his idols. Jesus was very concerned about materialism, and some of his most memorable stories and illustrations warning about "mammon" and filthy lucre stick in our minds. Remember his metaphor about a camel going through the eye of a needle (Mark 10:25)?

Some people think that money is evil, but it is neutral. It is merely a tool, the power to get other people to do things for us or to acquire things. It is the *love* of money that makes us sick. The Bible both warns about money sickness but at the same time encourages us to work hard and acquire wealth. It is not wrong to seek to build your family's financial security: **"The blessing of the Lord brings wealth"** (Proverbs 10:22). **"The righteous are rewarded with good things"** (Proverbs 13:21). **"All hard work brings a profit"** (Proverbs 14:23).

One of the best ways to do both things—build wealth and avoid sinful materialism—is to be generous with God and with people. **"Honor the Lord with your wealth, with the firstfruits of your crops; then your barns will be filled to overflowing"** (Proverbs 3:9,10). If you don't cheat and are generous with God and others, remembering and honoring the great Giver of all you have, God is happy that you can enjoy the bounty of his earth, which after all *he created for people*, did he not? **"The wise store up choice food and olive oil"** (Proverbs 21:20).

5

"Do not fear, for I have redeemed you; I have summoned you by name; you are mine" (Isaiah 43:1).

Why Does Bad Stuff Happen?

Q: When there are floods and massive fires in parts of the world, are these signs of the end times? Is God trying to tell us something?

A: Yes to both. Just like Lot's wife (Genesis 19:26), all of us are susceptible to the addiction of falling in love with this present age. As bad as Sodom was, Lot's wife managed to look away from the violence and corruption and look longingly at its pleasures and delights. Shortsightedness is a universal human failing. God allows violent disruptions of our dreamy status quo so that we will be reminded that this earth will one day be destroyed and rebuilt. What a disaster if the end should catch us unaware.

Jesus spent a lot of time teaching his disciples to have that long-term awareness: **"You will hear of wars and rumors of wars, but see to it that you are not alarmed. Such things must happen, but the end is still to come. Nation will rise against nation, and kingdom against kingdom.** *There will be famines and earthquakes* **in various places. All these are the beginning of birth pains"** (Matthew 24:6-8).

Natural disasters are not of recent origin. The earth has been shaking and starving and flooding and howling with severe storms for millennia. But each natural catastrophe can help believers go through their readiness drill. As fond as we are of Planet Earth, we need to accept that it is slated for demolition and rebuilding.

God is trying to tell us something—to be ready: **"The day of the Lord will come like a thief. The heavens will disappear with a roar; the elements will be destroyed by fire, and the earth and everything done in it will be laid bare. Since everything will be destroyed in this way, what kind of people ought you to be? You ought to live holy and godly lives as you look forward to the day of God and speed its coming. That day will bring about the destruction of the heavens by fire, and the elements will melt in the heat"** (2 Peter 3:10-12).

What if today is The Day?

• • • • • • •

Q: Are natural disasters acts of God or the devil? Can the devil control the weather?

A: As much as we pastors want people to be terrified of Satan and the mortal dangers of his lies, we can take some small comfort that he is not on God's level. He was made a creature. He is not God's peer. He is not omnipotent. Though he is a powerful demon, insanely mightier than we frail mortals, he only *thinks* he is lord of the earth. He isn't. He can counterfeit some of God's miracles, as the wizards in pharaoh's court partially imitated Moses' supernatural gifts with demonic help (Exodus 7:11,22). But he does not give orders to creation.

Nature turns on the people who live in it because nature itself is sick. When Adam and Eve first rebelled, they invited not only disease, war, famine, and death to plague the human race. They brought in a planetary virus of some sort that disrupted the earth's functions. St. Paul says that the whole world is breaking down: **"The creation waits in eager expectation for the children of God to be revealed. For the creation was subjected to frustration, not by its own choice, but by the will of the one who subjected it, in hope that the creation itself will be liberated from its** *bondage to decay* **and brought into the freedom and glory of the children of God"** (Romans 8:19-21).

If the rocks and rivers could talk, they would say how eager they are for judgment day, for then they will be free of the forces of evil that warp them. In the new heaven and new earth that God will create, nature will never again turn on its inhabitants to destroy and kill. It will be healthy again.

● ● ● ● ● ● ●

Q: How can a God who is supposed to be so good allow so much pain in the world?

A: "Supposed to be good"? Did you say, "*Supposed* to be good?"

What does our God need to do to establish the fact of the purity and goodness of his divine heart? Does not the splendor, complexity, and vastness of his created universe show you that he likes you so much that he wanted to provide an interesting and beautiful place for you to live? Does not the sight of Christ on his cross, bloody and dying, show you the great value that he places on you, that he literally gave his all to win you back? Doesn't the ceaseless working of the Holy Spirit show you his goodness? He personally provided the content and motivation and authors to give you the sacred Scripture, the only source of information that reveals the one true answer to the riddle of human existence.

Human beings suffer because God gave us significance. He gave us the dignity of causality, i.e., what we do *really matters.* Our actions can cause great joy and pleasure for others; they can also cause great pain. If you wish to shine a spotlight on the cause of human misery, point it at us. *We have done this to ourselves.* It's like a parent who tells her children over and over in January, "Don't put your tongue on the metal porch railing." Of course that makes putting your tongue on a metal porch railing in winter something desirable. If the children foolishly do that, fairness demands that they accept responsibility for their misery. God didn't make people invite catastrophe and pain and death to the world. We did it.

God in mercy does many things to relieve human suffering in our lives. He reveals the secrets of the construction of the human body and guides scientists to discover drugs and technologies that extend life. He surrounds us with friends and loved ones who help us bear our burdens. He assures us of his love and forgiveness through Word and sacrament so that we won't despair.

On the cross of Christ, God went all in to relieve human suffering—he struck a mighty blow that once and for all defeated evil and sin and hell and Satan. On the cross Jesus paid the price to unlock the golden gates of Paradise, and all believers may enter. In that new world, human pain and suffering will be completely absent (Revelation 21:4). In this light you might say that human pain can be therapeutic— it leads us to pray to and trust our kind heavenly Father for his daily help; it steadily reminds us that this world is broken beyond repair; and it lifts up our eyes to heaven, our real home.

* * * * * * *

Q: Why do you think God doesn't always send his angels in to save the day, especially in cases of terrible natural disasters or things like school shootings?

A: Two thoughts on that urgent and aching question. The first is a gentle reminder that we are not in heaven yet. Nature is broken and it doesn't work right. So are the people—they're broken too. A school shooting shows what Satan is really like. You can't deny the existence of human evil when you hear and see those dreadful stories, and you can't deny the reality of the sick demonic influence that drove the violence. Imagine—armed madmen dragging innocent little bystanders into their personal drama of anger and revenge to make some kind of "powerful" statement. But know this—God did not do a single thing to cause such acts of violence. Nor was he the one who warped the forces of nature to turn on its inhabitants.

My second thought is to encourage you to acknowledge that God's angels have been busier than we will ever know. In mercy God *does* act to lessen the blows of nature's wildness and of human cruelty. But—it's hard to notice a negative. In other words, if something *didn't* happen, you didn't notice it. We will be amazed to find out in heaven, if God lets us see his heavenly security tapes, about how many hundreds of thousands of times the angels *did* stop something bad from happening. We just didn't notice it *because it never happened.*

Let me invite you to trust and believe that God's angels

are deployed and working miracles on your behalf. **"The angel of the Lord encamps around those who fear him, and he delivers them"** (Psalm 34:7).

• • • • • • •

Q: What is God's will on war and the commandment "thou shall not kill"?

A: You are quoting the Fifth Commandment (Exodus 20:13) from the King James Version of the Bible, completed in the year A.D. 1611. A study of the original Hebrew verb in verse 13, *ratzach*, suggests that the Fifth Commandment is better translated, "You shall not *murder*." Most contemporary English Bible translations use that reading. There is a big difference between killing and murdering. You can't have a military without the capability and readiness to kill. You can't arm a police force unless its officers are allowed to use their weapons.

The Fifth Commandment does not forbid killing per se. Hunting and butchering animals for food is killing, but it is not a sin. Using deadly force in defense of your home and life is not a sin. God forbids murder, which is the taking of *innocent* life. He has empowered legitimate governments with his own divine authority to establish order, keep the peace, punish evildoers, and provide for national defense.

Here are St. Paul's powerful words: **"Let everyone be subject to the governing authorities, for there is no authority except that which God has established. The authorities that exist have been established by God. Consequently, whoever rebels against the authority is rebelling against what God has instituted, and those who do so will bring judgment on themselves. For rulers** hold no terror for those who do right, but for those who do wrong. Do you want to be free from fear of the one in authority? Then do what is right and you will be commended. For the one in authority is God's servant for your good. But if you do wrong, be afraid, for *rulers do not bear the sword for no reason.* They are *God's servants, agents of wrath* to bring punishment on the wrongdoer" (Romans 13:1-4).

In a violent world, government agents must be prepared to use deadly force to deter or stop violent evildoers. We don't use swords anymore, so if written today verse 4 might have mentioned guns. Military personnel, police officers, and prison guards who carry out capital punishment are not breaking the Fifth Commandment in the legitimate execution of their duties.

Warfare should always be a last resort of self-defense, not a means to annex territory or benefit from spoils. The God who empowers governments to bear arms will also hold them accountable for how they use their great power.

● ● ● ● ● ● ●

Q: Psalm 121:7 says, **"The Lord will keep you from all harm."** How is this true when historically and even in the present day, Christians are being harmed and even martyred endlessly? Christians were fed to the lions in Rome, many of Jesus' own disciples were killed for their faith, and present-day Christians are persecuted. How does this Scripture reconcile with these facts?

A: This psalm does not pretend to teach that there will be heaven on earth. Only after the great judgment day will violence and danger disappear for good. In the meantime, they are parts of our life experience while we are here.

What Psalm 121:7 is telling us is that *God intervenes in human history* to restrain Satan and all his violent human helpers and averts physical and emotional harm to the believers. Think of Daniel spending a nervous night in a pit with starving lions; or Shadrach, Meshach, and Abednego standing in a fiery furnace but remaining unharmed. They were kept from all harm in those circumstances. Why? Because their rescue served God's agenda and because he had more work for them all to do.

But sometimes heroes of faith served God by martyrdom. Daniel escaped mauling by lions, but John the Baptist did not escape the beheader's ax. The apostle James also was beheaded, and Stephen the deacon was stoned to death. In each case God made an assessment of what would most help advance the growth of his kingdom. Allowing these loyal servants to be persecuted and killed was not a disaster for them—it only propelled them into eternal glory faster.

Since we don't know the details of what God is up to at any given moment, we will always pray for deliverance. Psalm 121 urges us to lift up our eyes to the hills, to the Maker of heaven and earth. It is a safe place to entrust our lives into his hands. If he still has work for us to do, we are behind his iron shield of protection and nothing can lay a glove on us. If our work is done and our time is up, we win even bigger—we go to our real home in heaven.

●　●　●　●　●　●　●

Q: How do we balance wanting to keep our children and families safe while also feeling called to show Christian love to those like refugees of war or registered sex offenders?

A: You've already partly answered your own question by using the word *balance*. You have elegantly summarized yet another of the paradoxes of the Christian life—the imperatives of living courageously and yet prudently. They are both urgent. They are also difficult to sort out. It's one thing to live and travel like St. Paul—free and single, no wife or children—and take risks in proclaiming the gospel. It is another to drag your family into a life situation that puts them at risk. I suspect that if Paul had been a husband and father he might not have been beaten and imprisoned as often. Not that he lacked courage, but he might have tried to avoid making his wife a widow and his children orphans.

Happily you are probably not the first person in your state or in your church body to contemplate some form or risk in service. Talk to the professionals, whether mission administrators or social service lifers. Do your homework. Assess the real risk; don't just go on impressions gleaned from one sensationalist TV show or from rumors. Connect with other people who have gone before you and done the same thing. Investigate escape strategies—if the adventure is not going well, how can you back out with the least damage?

Spend serious time on this with your spouse. Any type of family risk should not move forward even one inch unless the husband and wife are agreed and share a passion for the mission. Listen to your kids. They may have surprising insights. And finally, don't make a move without taking the whole enterprise to God's throne in prayer. His answer probably won't come written in the sky above your head. It will come more likely as a feeling in your insides, either one of apprehension (No) or mission burn (Yes).

6

"This is the confidence we have in approaching God: that if we ask anything according to his will, he hears us"
(1 John 5:14).

Prayer

Q: I have a hard time making up my own prayers, but I don't really feel like I'm talking to God when I recite formal prayers either.

A: I've got to say that's really perceptive of you to be so self-aware, and also honest. If both spontaneous and printed prayers aren't working for you, your prayer life must be a struggle. Let's talk.

When you feel awkward in speaking your own prayers, try some of these things:

- Visualize God smiling at you. Imagine the Ancient of Days on his throne. Imagine the Son of God, our Savior Jesus, at his right hand and they're both actually *smiling* at you. And imagine the radiance and glory of the Holy Spirit just coming down in peace, coming like rays of sunlight and warming your face. Know that through Jesus you are dear and welcome in God's presence.

- You don't have to pretend to be somebody else. He likes you as is and loves to hear from you. Are you a parent? You know how you love it when your kids talk to you?

Your heavenly Father loves it when you come and talk to him. Even if you stammer, even if you hem and haw a little, even if it's not polished prose that some editor has tuned up, he likes to hear from you in whatever way the words come out. You can't bore him or disappoint him or fail him as you pray.

- Just let the thoughts come out. Take your time. You're not on the clock. He's not offended by stretches of silence as you come up with your next thoughts.

- Make a few bullet points of what it is that you want to communicate. Maybe you want to say thank you. Itemize the things that you're grateful for. Maybe you need forgiveness for what a dope you've been or some residual guilt that's hanging over your head like a dark cloud. Jot that down too. Or maybe you've got some things you need, or you want to call his divine attention to someone in your family who needs help. Write them down in little phrases to help you remember and then if you need to, refer to your notes when you pray. God doesn't mind.

- If spontaneous praying is hard for you, keep 'em short. You get no merit points for lengthy and windy discourses. Start with one-sentence prayers and then say Amen. Bang. You're done. Tomorrow you can try for two sentences. Later . . .

I know what you mean about printed prayers. I've read some out loud in worship situations that sure didn't sound like me. But not every prayer in a prayer book is necessarily meant to be uttered from your mouth. You can read through them and learn of the struggles and triumphs of other believers. You can learn from the way they talk and find some that have your voice. They can inform you how to talk to God even if they don't always bring the content you want. You can take a yellow marker as you go through a prayer book and highlight the ideas that you would like to utter to God and then stitch a prayer together with those authentic thoughts.

● ● ● ● ● ● ●

Q: Why does it take so long for God to answer some of my prayers?

A: I notice that you say "some" of your prayers. The inference is that other prayers of yours have been answered right away. Marvelous! One of those that God always answers right away is the prayer for forgiveness and spiritual cleansing and healing. He never makes us wait for that. But you are correct; sometimes God's answer to our prayers is *no*, and sometimes his answer to our prayers is *maybe* or *later* or *depends; we'll see*. In fact, sometimes I think God acts very much like my own parents. I can still remember my parents saying those very same things to me.

We can't hear a direct response from him, so we're not aware if this is going to be a right-away answer or not. Is this going to be a later answer? A maybe answer, depending on what I choose or do or how I act; or is it a no? We have to wait and see what he is going to do.

Why does it take so long for God to move? God doesn't think he takes long at all. From his point of view every action that he takes is right on time. It absolutely fits with his time line and agenda for what he wants to happen in our lives. God always acts in our best interest for his ultimate goal—to lead us to believe in him so that we will survive the severe finality of the last judgment, survive the physical destruction of the universe, and have a place to live with him in the new world that he is going to create.

And whether or not we are famous or wealthy or live long on this earth may or may not be helpful to that agenda. We'll cut him some slack to let him decide when and how to act on our prayers. Every prayer does get answered; it's just that answer may be a deferment. Or he may act right away and start changing things, but we can't see those movements. We will only see the final result.

Sometimes God waits to be asked again. That doesn't mean that there's something wrong with you. God doesn't mind repeat requests. When my children were small, if they would ask me for something I thought inappropriate and I said no but they asked me three times in the same day, the third time they might get yelled at for annoying me. But God doesn't see things that way. He sometimes intentionally delays a response in order to spur us and stimulate us to come back and ask again (watch Jesus in action doing that very thing in Mark 7:24-30). The Bible tells us that God *loves* persistent prayer (see Luke 18:1-8). So come back and ask again. You are not insulting his intelligence. It's not that he forgot what you brought up yesterday and now you need to remind him. But he loves to see you grow in your determination and intensity.

And sometimes he will say yes to you, even if it wasn't in his original plan. He says yes to you *just because you asked.* Sometimes I think God is intentionally holding onto a great bundle of blessings for you in his arms, but he's waiting for you to talk to him. With great joy he will then start dropping blessings on your life.

• • • • • • •

Q: Does God wait for a certain amount of people to pray before he does something (heals someone, etc.)?

A: We have only guesses and speculation as to why God may wait or delay acting on one of our requests. Do multiple petitioners make it more likely that the prayer will be answered? The Bible does not speak directly to your question. But I know for sure that, as much as he loves to hear our personal prayers, God loves group intercession as well. Jesus said once, **"Truly I tell you that if two of you on earth agree about anything they ask for, it will be done for them by my Father in heaven. For where two or three gather in my name, there am I with them"** (Matthew 18:19,20). Jesus earnestly wanted and needed prayer support from his three leading disciples in the Garden of Gethsemane (but appeared not to get it).

When you have issues in your life that are weighing you down, ask your family for prayer help around the dinner table. Ask your wider family for their intercessions on your behalf. If it's not too private and personal, ask your church and its small groups to pray for you.

• • • • • • •

Q: How do you deal with unanswered prayers when it seems as though God does not care?

A: In your haze of frustration and pain, Satan has persuaded you to believe two lies. First, that God doesn't care about you. Wrong! His desire to live with you and love you forever is behind the entire majestic plan of salvation that took thousands of years to unfold. **"He who did not**

spare his own Son, but gave him up for us all—how will he
not also, along with him, graciously give us all things?"
(Romans 8:32). You may confidently assume that every
action of God toward you is motivated by love.

Second, there is no such thing as an unanswered prayer
that comes from a Christian. God answers them all. We
like the "yes" answers; we chafe restlessly with the "later"
answers, and we don't like "no" answers at all. But God
invites you to trust his big view and full understanding that
sometimes no is better for you than yes. I ask my kids to
believe that of me; God asks us to believe that of him. Who
on earth loves my kids more than my wife and me? Who loves
his believing children more than our kind heavenly Father?

Let's cut our Father some slack. Just because he doesn't
do what we want does not prove that he's uncaring. We
have our own narrow little agendas; God has to weave his
interventions in human history into many lives. Our requests
could set off a chain reaction that would hurt other people—
only God can see wide enough and far enough ahead to juggle
many requests for him to change the course of history.

Sometimes our prayers ask for the wrong things and
we just can't see it at the time. The Christian people of the
Southern states from 1861 to 1865 devoutly and passionately
prayed for military triumph for the Confederate armies. I am
personally grateful that the pro-slavery faction in America
did not prevail.

God's ways often seem murky and confusing to us now.
That's okay. He tells us what we need to know and asks us to
leave the rest to him. But he promises that someday soon we
will get it: **"Now we see only a reflection as in a mirror; then
we shall see face to face. Now I know in part; then I shall
know fully, even as I am fully known"** (1 Corinthians 13:12).

* * * * * * *

Q: Why does the Lord's Prayer say "lead us not into temptation" when our Lord would never do that?

A: James chapter 1 shows us that God never tempts anyone to sin; he hates the very notion. James writes, **"When tempted, no one should say, 'God is tempting me.' For God cannot be tempted by evil, nor does he tempt anyone; but each person is tempted when they are dragged away by their own evil desire and enticed. Then, after desire has conceived, it gives birth to sin; and sin, when it is full-grown, gives birth to death"** (verses 13–15). The five little words in the Sixth Petition of the Lord's Prayer are shorthand for a plea that God would have mercy on us because of our many sinful weaknesses and keep us from committing spiritual suicide. We are all prone to becoming careless, stubborn, hard of hearing, and reckless in the way we live; and we must keep imploring God to send his angels of protection.

The Bible is a mighty resource to keep us out of temptation. It is armor for our hearts and a helmet for our brains. I hope you read some of it each day. Jesus himself was directed by his Father to live for over a month in the harsh conditions of the Judean wilderness as his ministry began. When he was at his physically weakest, Satan came at him with attractive lies, attractive challenges, and attractive offers. Jesus fought him off (successfully) three times. How? By zapping him with blue electrical fire coming from his hands? By levitating him back to the lowest pit of hell? Nope. By rebuking him with three words from Scripture. **"Submit yourselves, then, to God. Resist the devil, and he will flee from you"** (James 4:7).

God also sends other Christian people into your life—listen to them when they speak words of warning to you. And one of God's greatest gifts of protection to you is your congregation. If you have one, cherish it and thank God for the strength you draw from it. Your pastor cares about your spiritual well-being, prays for your safe journey, and will help you watch out for the ditches.

* * * * * * *

Q: When bad things happen in our world, there's suddenly a call for prayer. People who don't even believe in God look to him for help. I know for a fact that God hears my prayers, but does God hear an unbeliever's prayer?

A: God *hears* everything that goes on in the world. That does not mean that he feels an obligation to change his course of action because an unbeliever asked him to. God refuses to be treated like an ATM machine—that you go through a protocol when you want something and then ignore it until the next crisis.

Jesus told his disciples on Maundy Thursday evening in the upper room that he alone is the Way, the Truth, and the Life, that nobody comes to the Father except through him (John 14:6). God obligates himself to his children in a way that he does not for unbelievers, and that includes people who participate in some of the outward trappings of Christianity but do not have faith in their hearts. Jesus' words about spiritual hypocrisy are chilling: **"Not everyone who says to me, 'Lord, Lord,' will enter the kingdom of heaven, but only the one who does the will of my Father who is in heaven. Many will say to me on that day, 'Lord, Lord, did we not prophesy in your name and in your**

name drive out demons and in your name perform many miracles?' Then I will tell them plainly, 'I never knew you. Away from me, you evildoers!'"
(Matthew 7:21-23).

As a believer, you can come to God and he *will* change his course of action *just because you asked*.

● ● ● ● ● ● ●

Q: How can I be sure that I'm praying according to God's will?

A: That is the right question to be asking! Notice that Jesus puts that in a trio of important attitudes and agenda items in his Lord's Prayer before we get to the fun things like daily bread and the gift of the forgiveness of your many sins. Hallowing God's name, praying and working for the kingdom, and dialing into God's will are *top* priorities for all Christians. It's not that you aren't supposed to pray for daily bread and all the other comforts and treats we desire. God loves to give you things. But *first things first*.

To discern God's will, don't look at the world around you, don't gaze inwardly at your own thoughts and emotions, don't consult psychics or read horoscopes, and don't sit quietly in meditation waiting for insights and impulses. Just get to know your Bible really well. Only through the Bible can you be sure of who God is. Only through the Bible can you be sure what he has done in history and what it means, and only through the Bible will you hear clear instructions for the church and for your personal mission on earth.

These are some of the things that spiritual leaders prayed about and urged others to pray about:

- Ezra 6:10: Pray for the king.

- Psalm 69:13: Pray for personal rescue and deliverance.

- Matthew 26:31: Pray that you won't fall into temptation.

- Matthew 5:44: Pray for those who persecute you.

- 3 John 1:2: Pray for good health for others.

- Ephesians 6:19: Pray for courage in pastors, missionaries, and teachers.

- Colossians 4:3: Pray for open doors for the message of the gospel.

- Colossians 1:3: Pray for your congregation.

You don't need prompts and reminders and Post-it notes to remember to pray for financial resources from God. But it might be a good idea to keep a prayer journal where you lay out your prayer agenda, name names, and plan a balanced prayer life. It could be a great spiritual exercise for a year.

• • • • • • • •

Q: Is there a proper way to pray?

A: The only requirements are that you direct your information to God in heaven, praying through the wonderful intercession of your Savior Jesus Christ.

God loves hearing from you whether you're kneeling, standing, sitting, driving in your car, or lying in your bed. He loves hearing from you whether it's morning, noon, or night; whether you think the thoughts, whisper them, say them out loud, or sing them in a Christian song. Your prayers can be short or long, formal or informal, in any language (he speaks them all), and uttered from any point on the earth or sky or even from outer space, if you happen to be an astronaut. Your prayers can be improvised and spontaneous, or you can read the devotional words of Scripture like the psalms as your personal prayers. You can read devotions and prayer books that provide you with a written message. They can be at a regularly scheduled time or just blurted out as the need arises.

- Your messages to God can be pure *worship* because of his glory, perfection, holiness, and love.

- Your messages can be *praises* because of the magnificent works he has done in creation, redemption, and spiritual transformation of people.

- Your messages can be *intercession* for the needs of others.

- Your messages can be *penitential*, calling for God's mercy on a sinner like you.

- Your messages can be *requests* for personal help. You can ask for anything you think you need. He will figure out if it's really good for you and when and how it will be delivered.

● ● ● ● ● ● ●

Q: What does it mean to pray in Jesus' name?

A: Christians love to end their prayers like this: "We ask all these things in the name of Jesus." We do that because of Jesus' powerful promise the night before he died: **"Truly I tell you, my Father will give you whatever you ask in my name. . . . Ask and you will receive, and your joy will be complete"** (John 16:23,24). Asking "in the name of Jesus," however, is more than just appending a phrase including one of Jesus' proper names at the end of each prayer.

The *name* of God can indeed refer to his proper names, and the Bible lists quite a few. But when we pray "hallowed be your name," we are not just promising God that we will show respect to his proper names. We are declaring our faith in God's entire self-revelation through his Word. His "name" in this wider sense is the Bible's fuller description of God's identity and the glorious accounts of his mighty works and deeds.

When Jesus invites us to pray in his name, this includes praying with confidence because of the status of God's child that we possess through our faith in him. We aren't begging from an omnipotent heavenly stranger. We are talking to Daddy. We are showing that we believe his Word's promises that he loves us and loves to listen to us. We can come back to him over and over, knowing that our many sins are forgiven through the blood of the Lamb and that he will never renege on his promises or reject us if we come with a penitent heart.

Praying in Jesus' name also means praying in alignment with Jesus' mission. It means paying attention to Jesus' teaching and instructions so that we know our role and work in the world. We can't expect God to agree with requests that would hurt other people or advance Satan's destructive work.

Ask and you will receive, and your joy will be complete!

• • • • • • •

Q: Why do most prayers end with the word *Amen*?

A: It is purely a custom. You are under no biblical or divine mandate to put that tiny little word at the end of every one of your prayers. In church we are under no command to put the word at the end of liturgical prayers and hymns. But it is a sweet custom. When you say or sing it, you are putting your stamp of approval on what you just heard, said, or sang.

It is part of the New Testament Greek vocabulary, which borrowed it from a much older Hebrew usage occurring about a dozen times in the Old Testament. The Hebrew word *Amen* is built off a root Hebrew verb that means "to be supported, propped, sustained, built up." *Amen* became an adverb that means "Truly!" It signifies your assent with the words of another (ideally you don't say "Amen" to your own statements).

I know that we often end our own prayers with *Amen*, and in our contemporary usage it functions like a period at the end of a sentence, or the way people used to dictate "Stop" to end a telegram. But the most proper way to use the word is for a worshiping group to endorse the content of a statement or prayer.

In Deuteronomy chapter 27, Moses instructed the people of Israel to go to Mounts Ebal and Gerizim and carry out a large-scale drama of committing themselves to shunning what God called sin and embracing what God called good. After a chorus of Levites spoke the instructions of the Lord, the people were to shout out "Amen!" after each sentence to demonstrate their approval.

One of the book of Revelation's most interesting metaphorical names for Jesus is "The Amen" (3:14), that is, the one who is the truth, speaks the truth, teaches the truth. The book ends, **"Amen. Come, Lord Jesus"** (22:20).

* * * * * * *

Q: What sorts of prayers can we pray for unbelievers?

A: I'm so delighted to hear this question! It is a refreshing antidote to this self-absorbed prayer you may have heard before: "Dear God, bless father and mother, sister and brother. These four. No more. Amen."

Of course Christians need to pray for those outside the faith. God loves unbelievers too, showering them with the bounties of the earth. His rainfall falls on their farms too. When the people of Israel, God's chosen covenant people, were removed from their ancient land and taken into captivity in Babylon, God did not want them committing acts of sabotage and rebellion. He wanted them to be great citizens of their new realm and to care about the people around them: **"Seek the peace and prosperity of the city to which I have carried you into exile. Pray to the LORD for it, because if it prospers, you too will prosper"** (Jeremiah 29:7).

We do need to care about the people in our faith communities, but God invites us to a much bigger worldview: **"Therefore, as we have opportunity, let us do good to *all* people, especially to those who belong to the family of believers"** (Galatians 6:10). What to pray for in the wider world?

- *Good governance.* Not all of the legislators who make the rules for your world are Christians. God steers governments small and great for the good of his agenda. You can pray especially for governments in non-Christian lands, that they will not persecute Christian churches and allow the free course of proclaiming and sharing the Word of God.

- *Peace.* Without God's restraining hand on Satan and his agents, our violent world would get even more hellish.

- *Faith in Christ* for them. Every time you pray the Lord's Prayer and ask God that his kingdom come, you are praying that the power of the Holy Spirit would turn more and more people to faith in Christ.

7

*"In him we have redemption through his blood,
the forgiveness of sins, in accordance with
the riches of God's grace" (Ephesians 1:7).*

Sin, Forgiveness, and Salvation

Q: Is sin just a myth?

A: Mary Baker Eddy, the founder of the Christian Science movement, certainly thought so. She wrote in her book *Science and Health*, "Matter, sin, and sickness are not real, but only illusions." A great many people today, including some who call themselves "spiritual," don't accept its reality either. They view such talk as hopelessly old school and want to get on with more interesting topics, such as freedom and liberation and empowerment.

Understanding what God means by "sin" begins at Genesis chapter 1. People who believe in evolution do not see themselves as God's divine creation. They don't accept the historical reality of Adam and Eve and their fall. They don't accept the presence of a universal moral code of conduct that the Creator has imposed on all humanity. They do not see themselves as subject to God's will, have no interest in the Ten Commandments, and reject any notion that God should be evaluating the morality of their lives. They are interested in the concepts of "truth" and "error" only insofar as they will allow that each individual may set up his or her own private morality, none of which is applicable to anybody else.

And then there is God's world, aka reality. Even without the Bible, even blind people can see the painful reality of universal evil all around us. Every victim of burglary, sexual assault, racism, and mugging is revolted by this direct contact with the agents of hell doing Satan's work of mayhem, chaos, and heartless cruelty. There's more: the voice of the conscience that God placed within us bears witness to the truth that there is evil within us too. This explains the thoughts, words, and actions that are at odds with God's law.

Don't rationalize your sin. Don't ignore it, blame others, pretend it's nothing, brag about it, or compare yourself to people worse than you. Just admit it to God: **"If we claim to be without sin, we deceive ourselves and the truth is not in us. If we confess our sins, he is faithful and just and will forgive us our sins and purify us from all unrighteousness. If we claim we have not sinned, we make him out to be a liar and his word is not in us"** (1 John 1:8-10).

Sin is real. But so is our Savior Jesus who takes it away.

● ● ● ● ● ● ●

Q: How can we know if something is a sin?

A: That's actually a deeper question than it may first appear. People have all kinds of religious information in their heads, but not all of it is solid gold.

Some religious laws they think they must obey are actually just urban legends; some are family sayings repeated through the generations; some are denominational traditions that have taken on the authority of divine law; some are their own interpretations and ideas.

If you want to know with certainty the will of God and the divine laws that you must obey, consult the New Testament. That is the "constitution" under which we live. The Old Testament is a treasury of information revealed by God, but many of the laws governing religious and social life were intended for Israel only and were intended to sunset at the coming of the Messiah. Those "sunsetted" laws include the kosher food rules and the no-work rules for Saturday, the Jewish Sabbath.

Some of the Old Testament moral instruction, such as the listing of the Ten Commandments in Exodus chapter 20, has been repeated and incorporated into the New Covenant. The Ten do provide a wonderfully concise way of remembering how God wants us to treat him and treat each other.

Listen to the voices of Christ in the gospels and the apostles in the letters and you will know God's will for your life. Believe and teach no more and no less than what you find there: **"I warn everyone who hears the words of the prophecy of this scroll: If anyone adds anything to them, God will add to that person the plagues described in this scroll. And if anyone takes words away from this scroll of prophecy, God will take away from that person any share in the tree of life and in the Holy City, which are described in this scroll"** (Revelation 22:18,19).

* * * * * * *

Q: Am I truly saved even though I continue to sin sometimes?

A: That cry from the heart is a common experience for all Christians, including St. Paul: **"I know that good itself does not dwell in me, that is, in my sinful nature. For I have the**

desire to do what is good, but I cannot carry it out. . . . Who will rescue me from this body of death?" (Romans 7:18,24). It is a hard truth that sin will live within us until we are raised up on judgment day and personally transformed in body and soul. In heaven we will never sin again, nor even desire to do so.

In the meantime, we find ourselves in the middle of a war. But it's a war that Christ *has already won.* The Holy Spirit has brought you to faith in Christ, and that means you are connected to all of his saving work on your behalf. When your sins trouble you (as they should), look not to yourself, your worth, your record, your achievements, nor even your good intentions, but look to the cross of Christ. Who will rescue us from this body of death? Jesus did.

We strive for holy living, but we should not pursue the illusion that we can achieve moral perfection this side of heaven. People who go that route either turn into smug Pharisees, unaware of the corruption within, or depressed and despairing ex-believers who are overwhelmed with their failures.

Jesus' death once and for all paid your obligations in God's court. You are declared not guilty. With that triumphant verdict and with new confidence you can return to the battle, seeking to honor God with your life for his matchless gift of a Savior. When you fall, repent. When you fall again, repent again. Repeat as needed. Remember that your salvation is based on Jesus' achievements, not yours. Soon comes heaven and the divine transformation, and then we will sin no more.

• • • • • • •

Q: Is there any sin that you could commit against God that he will not forgive?

A: See comments on the earlier question about the "sin against the Holy Spirit" on page 33.

The Bible is painfully honest in sharing information about human brokenness and evil. Even the great heroes of faith have sinful episodes in their lives laid out in humiliating detail. Abraham compounded his adultery with Hagar by driving her and her young "illegitimate" son Ishmael out into the desert. Though Abraham was a wealthy man by that time, the two were forced out of his household with only enough food for one meal (Genesis 21:8-20). David's long string of moral failures with Bathsheba, including covetousness, lies, theft, and the arranged military assassination of her legitimate husband, are made public for all generations of believers to see (2 Samuel 11).

But through the gospel these foolish sinners were restored to God's family and put back to work for the kingdom. Jesus even had mercy and forgiveness for the violent criminal crucified at his side. That unnamed malefactor is an endless source of hope and encouragement to sinners like you and me that the cleansing power of Jesus' blood is bigger than our ability to do evil. Think of it—the blood of God himself was shed on the cross! Kneel in awe and worship!

And not only are our worst sins pardoned through Christ, the mighty power of the Holy Spirit, working through Word and sacrament, is able to move our rebellious hearts to repentance, to faith in the Lamb, and to a new desire to start over and serve God with a clean heart.

So what is burdening your heart right now? You can't

scare or surprise God. Tell the truth. No excuses. No blaming. No minimizing. No rationalizing. Just back the truck up to Jesus' cross and dump the load. All of it. Hold nothing back. And then look up at your Savior and realize that it was for just such a time as this and for just such a person as you that he needed to live and die in this way. Worship him with all your mind and strength. And then show your gratitude by making some changes in the way you live.

Tomorrow you will need to repent again.

Tomorrow Jesus will forgive you again.

* * * * * * *

Q: I did a lot of bad things as a young man and lived a pretty rough life. I feel really bad about it. Jesus loves me, doesn't he? Does he forgive me? I hope and pray yes because when I die, I want more than ever to live in heaven with Jesus.

A: The last part of your life matters more than the first. If you lived like a choirboy as a young man and then gave up Christianity for the party life in your later years, it's your spiritual condition at the end of your life on which God will evaluate you. Similarly the wretched spiritual attitudes you had in your early life are not relevant now if you have repented of your sins. And that's the key.

People change. People who were loyal disciples of the Lord lose interest and quit the faith. People who lived like rebels catch spiritual fire late in life and do a 180. For one of the Bible's most astounding personal turnarounds, read the story of evil King Manasseh in 2 Chronicles chapter 33. He looked like a sure candidate for hell in his earlier realm, but things changed. He **"humbled himself greatly before the**

God of his ancestors" (verse 12). The violent criminal who was being executed next to Jesus came to his senses very late in the game and repented, and Jesus assured him that he was headed for Paradise.

St. Paul in his early adult life burned with a hot passion to persecute, arrest, and kill Christians. Can you imagine his regrets? But God mercifully kept him alive until he could change him around and light the fire of faith in his heart. Paul's painful memories were always with him, and they served to keep him humble and grateful for grace: **"Here is a trustworthy saying that deserves full acceptance: Christ Jesus came into the world to save sinners—of whom I am the worst. But for that very reason I was shown mercy so that in me, the worst of sinners, Christ Jesus might display his immense patience as an example for those who would believe in him and receive eternal life"** (1 Timothy 1:15,16).

If you are practicing justifying yourself in your mind in preparation for judgment day, you will always be nervous. There is just too much dirt in our lives. Don't look at yourself! Look at Jesus.

●　●　●　●　●　●　●

Q: Will God forgive me even if I can't forgive someone else?

A: I salute both your honesty and your awareness that you have a serious problem. You are asking the right question! It is an offense against the gospel if you take Jesus' forgiveness for yourself and refuse to give yours to another person.

This is a big deal. God's mercy is pure kinetic energy. It needs to be moving to do anybody any good. It needs to move into your mind and heart, assuring you that you have a Friend and Savior in Jesus. It needs to calm your guilty conscience, washing out the sin and replacing it with God's royal favor.

But God's mercy needs to keep moving—not only *to* you but *through* you. Jesus not only *invites* you to show kindness, patience, and a forgiving spirit to other fools and sinners around you (gospel), he actually *commands* you to do it and warns you that you risk forfeiting your own forgiveness if you withhold it from another (law). He calls that a *wicked* sin.

He told a powerful parable near the end of his ministry about a servant who was forgiven a massive debt but who harshly held on to a small IOU from a fellow servant. **"Then the master called the servant in. 'You *wicked* servant,' he said, 'I canceled all that debt of yours because you begged me to. Shouldn't you have had mercy on your fellow servant just as I had on you?' In anger his master handed him over to the jailers to be tortured, until he should pay back all he owed."** Jesus then concluded with this severe warning: **"This is how my heavenly Father will treat each of you unless you forgive your brother or sister from your heart"** (Matthew 18:32-35).

There are two levels of forgiveness. First comes the release of anger in your own heart. Let it go. No matter how badly you've been hurt in the past, God assures you of your beauty and worth in his eyes. Earthly things are passing away soon, and holding onto old grudges, grievances, and revenge fantasies will only poison your soul. No sin against you is so great that you would want to risk forfeiting your own forgiveness. Let it go. Look through the windshield of your life, not the rearview.

Second, a trickier level of forgiving is whether or not to speak your forgiveness to the person who hurt you (if that is even possible). The key is whether or not the person expresses remorse and asks for your forgiveness. Give it then (without trying to read the person's mind and spirit to ascertain whether or not he or she is sincere or not—you will never know that for sure). If the person is lying, faking, or playing manipulation games, give it to God to take care of and let it go.

Do it. Do it for Jesus' sake.

● ● ● ● ● ● ●

Q: How can God love me? I sin all the time.

A: You are viewing your relationship with God as a business transaction. You are assuming that God's love for you is tentative, that it depends on the quality of your love in return. You fear that his love is conditional and that you are probably disappointing him so much and so often that his affection will fade and perhaps is gone already.

God is indeed intensely interested in your life and behaviors. He wants to see acts of love and good deeds, but only as a grateful response to his love given to you first, *not as a condition that you must meet in order to secure his love for you!* He is perfectly happy to front you his mercy and forgiveness, trusting that you will respect and appreciate the sacrifice it took to give it to you.

The apostle John expressed the miracle of God's love for us more poignantly that anyone else:

"God is love. This is how God showed his love among us: He sent his one and only Son into the world that we might live through him. This is love: not that we loved God, but that he loved us and sent his Son as an atoning sacrifice for our sins" (1 John 4:8-10).

You are not endlessly falling out of God's family because

of your sins and then have to earn your way back in with atoning behaviors. Jesus did all the atoning necessary. Repent of your sins, all of them, big, medium, and small, and dump them on the ash heap at the foot of Jesus' cross. Claim the forgiveness that is yours and start afresh. Let your heart rejoice at all the pleasure you are giving to the Lord when you worship him, serve him, make people's lives better, and give him glory in your life.

Through Jesus' holiness now attributed to you, when you stand in line on judgment day, you will be astonished to hear, **"Well done, good and faithful servant! . . . Come and share your master's happiness"** (Matthew 25:21).

● ● ● ● ● ● ●

Q: How can I forgive my sister and have peace when it comes to her behavior?

A: Why does she irritate you so much? Does she know how to push all your fear buttons? Does she bring up your past failures? Does she make you feel stupid? Does she try to dominate you? Does she belittle your accomplishments? Does she think your hobbies and passions are silly? Does she think her children are superior to yours? Does she value your opinion?

Once you've found a way to put your angry feelings into words, sit down and write up a little list of the behaviors that you find hurtful. Why do you suppose she acts the way she does? Is she aware of how intensely she is frustrating you, or do you keep it bottled up? Is she really insecure and maybe trying to be bigger by making you smaller? Are the words and actions you can't stand something from the past or do they keep recurring?

Here are a few of the Proverbs that may have a little wisdom for your mind and heart:

- **"A gentle answer turns away wrath, but a harsh word stirs up anger"** (15:1).

- **"Where there is strife, there is pride"** (13:10).

- **"A kindhearted woman gains honor"** (11:16).

- **"Whoever seeks good finds favor, but evil comes to one who searches for it"** (11:27).

- **"Fools show their annoyance at once, but the prudent overlook an insult"** (12:16).

May you find the grace to turn the other cheek, return sharp words with soft words, let go of your anger, take her words and actions in the kindest possible way, refuse to bad-mouth her to others, and find things to praise in her. And may the love of the Lord so fill both your hearts that you are once again drawn close to each other.

* * * * * * *

Q: What is true repentance? I'm sorry that I keep on drinking too much, but yet I keep doing it.

A: Just so we understand each other—the sin is not in drinking alcohol. Alcohol itself is God's gift, and its use is up to each individual. Drinking becomes a sin when the person gets impaired or drunk, loses control of behavior, damages relationships, inappropriately operates a motor vehicle, damages his or her health, or becomes addicted. Problem drinkers usually do all of those things.

Repentance has three phases. Phase 1 is recognizing and admitting the sin. That's harder than it looks. The leaders of AA groups spend a lot of time helping problem drinkers admit that they are out of control and need to surrender. It may even take an intervention, where people who love the individual stand in a circle and confront him or her: "You're an alcoholic!" If you are a problem drinker, admit it to the people closest to you, people whom you've probably hurt in some way. Most important of all, admit it to God. Don't run away. Just tell the truth (unfortunately one of the first casualties when people become slaves of alcohol). Stop the games and pretending and lying and excusing.

Phase 2 is to claim the forgiveness that Jesus your Savior brings. He doesn't despise you for being weak. He just wants you to realize that you need his help. Let his love make you believe that you are still lovable. If he still has a use for you and hasn't given up on you, then you don't have to give up on yourself.

Phase 3 is to ask for the Spirit's help in making the changes you need to make. Do you need to quit completely? Ask your friends to help you stop—let them know so that they won't tempt you. Identify yourself as a teetotaler so that their eyes will be on you if you try to sneak one at a restaurant. Try some of the AA meetings in your town—their organization has a much higher success rate than most other options. They will tell you about a "higher power"—you know exactly who that is. Identify a buddy or mentor who has quit drinking as someone you can call when you feel the cravings beginning.

● ● ● ● ● ● ●

Q: How much faith do you need to be saved?

A: Your salvation is based not on the power or quantity

or longevity of your faith, but on what your faith is in. Your faith doesn't take away your sins; Jesus does. Your faith is just your connector to what really saves you.

Our faith will never be 100 percent. Sin, aging, and physical weaknesses cloud our brains, corrupt our memories, and distort our perceptions. Our spirits may be willing, but our flesh is tired and weak. A man with a son tormented by a demon approached Jesus for help: **"'It has often thrown him into fire or water to kill him. But if you can do anything, take pity on us and help us.' '"If you can"?' said Jesus. 'Everything is possible for one who believes.' Immediately the boy's father exclaimed, 'I do believe; help me overcome my unbelief!'"** (Mark 9:22–24). Don't torment yourself if you know you have some doubts.

Seven centuries before Christ, the prophet Isaiah had foretold that the coming Savior would have a gentle touch, that he would not despise the people he came to save or look down on them because they were broken, confused, and weak: **"A bruised reed he will not break, and a smoldering wick he will not snuff out"** (Matthew 12:20).

Don't play games with God's patience, though. The fact that he comes to you with a gentle knock on the door and an understanding heart does not mean that you can settle for any old kind of attitude toward him. Don't settle for minimums or see how little effort you can get away with or how close to the edge you can skate. You are in charge of your own spiritual feeding, accountable to God himself.

That's why he has given us such a powerful resource in his Word, the Bible. The Bible is a source of infallible information, a faith builder and strengthener, a light for your path, stiffness for your spine, wisdom for your soul, energy and pep for your step, and comfort for your last days. Listen. Read. Remember. Cherish.

*more straight*TALK

● ● ● ● ● ● ●

Q: Does faith grow on its own, or is it something you have to work at? How can you increase your faith?

A: Faith doesn't just drift around in the wind like yeast spores in search of something to ferment. You can't synthesize it by yourself. It doesn't jump from one person to another like a holy virus or bacterium. It comes to people in only one way—through the Word of God and through Baptism. St. Paul tells us in Romans 10:17, **"Faith comes from hearing the message, and the message is heard through the word of Christ."**

Now while you can't create or produce faith inside yourself, you can move your feet to places where the Word is in motion, and you can move your eyes on the page where that Word is to be found (as did the Ethiopian in Acts 8:26-39). The more you know of God's awesome identity and power, the more you will want to worship him. The more you hear of his mighty works, the more you will want to praise him. The more you know of the incredible work of Christ on your behalf, the more you will love him. The more you know of the patient and persistent working of the Spirit in your mind and heart, the more you will appreciate him.

The Word informs you about the meaning of what you see in your world and explains to you why things happen. The longer this growth in understanding and perception goes on, the stronger your faith will grow. Over the years you will see God proved right in everything his Word says. You will see your prayers answered, your doubts diminished, your confusion lessened, your fears eased, your heart comforted, your contentment increased, and your patience and endurance multiplied.

170

How can you increase your faith? Simple. Maximize your exposure to the Bible, the Word of God.

● ● ● ● ● ● ●

Q: Is salvation truly built on faith alone? I have a hard time believing that I don't have to do anything at all.

A: Set aside a few minutes, take out your Bible, and read Ephesians 2:1–10 slowly. Read it again. You will notice two powerful ideas in this critical portion of God's Word:

1. Your salvation is by God's *grace* alone, connected to you through *faith, not by works*.
2. Your new life of faith expresses itself *through* your good works.

"I don't have to do anything at all" is true only with reference to the question of how my sins got forgiven. It is Christ's blood, not yours, that washes you. It is Christ's performance, not yours, that you will claim on judgment day. It is Christ's riches, not your wages, that you want in your wallet. Whoever believes in him will not perish. **"David says the same thing when he speaks of the blessedness of the one to whom God *credits* righteousness *apart from works*: 'Blessed are those whose transgressions are forgiven, whose sins are covered'"** (Romans 4:6,7).

It cost you nothing to become a child of God. But it will cost you everything to live like one. Scripture invites us to offer ourselves back to God as *living sacrifices*, holy and pleasing to him (Romans 12:1). Go back to your Ephesians reading and gaze at the last verse: **"We are God's handiwork, created in Christ Jesus to do good works, which God prepared in advance for us to do."**

You were loved from all eternity, redeemed at great cost,

and caused to be reborn not so you could go back to the sty and live like a pig. The Spirit who now lives in you motivates you to worship God, work hard, love people, serve others' needs, care for your family, keep your word, and share your faith with the other strugglers and stragglers around you. God planned from all eternity to redeem you. He also from all eternity prepared a life of good works for you to do, and he expects you do them.

● ● ● ● ● ● ●

Q: I don't get the whole predestination thing. If God chose us, how could we ever fall away? Or how could some who were unbelievers come to faith?

A: An ancient complaint against the Bible is that God doesn't tell us enough—we want to know more.

Well, with the teaching of predestination (also called election), God let's you peek behind the curtain of how he does things. Suddenly we are swimming in very deep water. Please don't pressure yourself to think you must understand these things. God tells them to you to believe, not understand. You and I will have to wait till heaven to know fully (1 Corinthians 13:12).

The cause for our eternal destiny—whether saved or damned—is a paradox. If we are saved, Scripture urges us to give all glory to God. If sinners are condemned, it's their fault. Period. Does that sound like something of a contradiction? Yes, I guess it does.

There are no answers this side of heaven for questions such as these:

• Why did God choose some and not others? Isn't that favoritism?

- If you aren't chosen for heaven, then doesn't that actually condemn you to hell?

- Why do some people believe the gospel and others hear the same message and don't believe it?

- How can you tell who is predestined for heaven and who isn't?

All of God's elect will be saved. We don't know who those people are. We assume that if we believe in Christ we must be part of that blessed company. If people end up in hell, they chose it. Since people can fall away from faith that they once held, does that mean that even while in a state of grace they weren't truly part of the elect? Punt. I will let God unravel that for you when he's ready.

God tells you about election for only one reason—so that you give him 100 percent of the credit for finding, converting, and preserving you in his grace. He did not just choose the nice ones, the people who would turn out well. His reasons for his choosing are not to be found in our "good qualities." He made his decisions entirely for his own reasons: **"I will have mercy on whom I have mercy, and I will have compassion on whom I have compassion"** (Romans 9:15).

Make a list of questions that you have for God when you see him. In the meantime, fix your eyes on Jesus.

● ● ● ● ● ● ●

Q: How do I know if I've truly been born again?

A: Spiritual regeneration was a really confusing concept to a man named Nicodemus also. In John's gospel in chapter 3, Jesus had a conversation with this Pharisee who struggled with that idea of needing to be born again. Jesus told him that no one can enter the kingdom of God without being born again of *water and the spirit* (i.e., by being baptized). The reason? Sinful flesh gives birth to sinful flesh. It takes the Holy Spirit to give birth to the new spirit in a person (i.e., create faith in his or her heart).

If you're born an unbeliever, without a direct intervention from God you will stay, live, and die an unbeliever. But God changes people; he converts us. He turns us from unbelief to faith. It's all his doing, and in the New Testament age he does it with his powerful Word and his wonderful washing of Baptism, which is that same Word with water applied to a person's body. Jesus called it "being born again of water and the spirit."

Now you may or may not have memories of that transition, of the moment of your conversion from unbelief to faith, death to life. Sometimes it's very quiet and subtle, and sometimes it's explosive. Perhaps you have friends who remember a moment in their lives of dramatic spiritual turnaround. Others have had such a gradual transition that they couldn't put their finger on an exact moment, or it happened in childhood or even infancy out of reach of even the faintest memories.

The way in which you personally will know if you've been born again is by listening to God's Word. Do you believe it when God's Word tells you you're a sinner? Do you believe it when God's Word tells you that your Savior Jesus has paid the ultimate price to purchase full and free forgiveness for all of your sins? If you say yes to those two things, the regeneration and rebirth have already happened and you can enjoy your new identity. Let God's Word continue to feed you, encourage you, and guide you as you get involved in God's agenda.

● ● ● ● ● ● ●

Q: Is there such a thing as "once saved, always saved"? In other words, can you lose your salvation? Is there Scripture speaking for or against this doctrine?

A: If you would like to get a rip-roaring argument started between Christians of different faith traditions, just throw that concept out at a gathering and feel the heat. Sad to say, this point is one of the deep divides between denominations and schools of thought in the Christian world.

There are two important points to ponder on this very important question. The first is that God is rock steady in his purposes. His proper name, represented in our English translations as "the Lord," reveals him as a God of faithful grace, a God who chooses to love people based on *his* decision, not our performance. James 1:17 assures us that God does not change like shifting shadows. He will never give up on us and delights in showing mercy. The Bible's term *grace* always refers to God's unconditional, undeserved, unlimited love and mercy.

However—the Bible teaches that we are saved by grace *through faith* (Ephesians 2:8,9). Does that seem like a paradox? It is. Let it be. Whenever we try to make Scripture's words fit our logical systems, we start to twist the truth. The truth is that Adam and Eve had the ability to reject God's love, and we do too. How could that be? Why would we? I think God himself is puzzled by that rejection. What's not to like about forgiveness of sins and everlasting life?

From God's point of view, it is so extremely important that we *give* our love and worship to him that he allows the possibility that we would *not* give him our love and worship. This is not a sign of fickleness or weakness on his part. In fact, it is a sign of the great respect that he shows us that he allows us a meaningful role in such high-stakes business. Our life choices have eternal consequences.

Here is what the Bible says about the capacity of human beings to throw away their faith: **"It is impossible for those who have once been enlightened, who have tasted the heavenly gift, who have shared in the Holy Spirit, who have tasted the goodness of the word of God and the powers of the coming age and who have fallen away, to be brought back to repentance"** (Hebrews 6:4-6). Suicide is a sad part of life in this world. So, alas, is spiritual suicide.

Is it possible to fall away? Yes. This is a sobering preaching of God's law. Jesus himself said this would happen for some. In his parable of the sower (Matthew 13:1-23), Jesus used the metaphor of crops to show that some plants (i.e., people) spring up and grow for a while, but weeds and rocks (Satan's temptations and distractions) over time stunt and kill the plants. This is no fault of the sower's high-quality seed (i.e., the Word of God).

Is it possible to fall away? Yes. But I'm not worried about you. *The very fact that you care about God's opinion of you shows that you are still a believer.* If you had lost your faith, you wouldn't care. When you are troubled by your sins and aware of your moral failings, repent of them and go to Christ's cross. His blood to cleanse is more powerful than your ability to stain. His power to remove guilt is greater than your power to pile it up. If you sin again, even the very same sin, repent again. And again. His mercy is new and fresh every morning. Our salvation is based on Christ's all-sufficient work, not our often-weak faith.

Feed that faith with Word and the Lord's Supper. Choose your friends carefully. Surround yourself with other

Christians in a Bible-based faith community. Above all, keep your eyes fixed on Jesus, the author and perfecter of our faith (Hebrews 12:2).

● ● ● ● ● ● ●

Q: How is it possible that the sins of the whole world could be paid for by the punishment and death of one person, even though that person is also God, when my own sins are as numerous as the grains of sand on a beach? Will you help me remove this nagging doubt?

A: The reason that there are nagging doubts is that at least partly you are looking at yourself for reasons for your salvation. Don't. Everything about our spiritual nature has flaws in it, and those flaws will drain away your confidence if you think that even in part you have to earn or deserve your place in heaven. You have an enemy in hell who will whisper to you every day that you are a worthless failure. Satan loves to tempt you to sin, and then he loves to taunt you and remind you of your weaknesses. Tell him to get lost.

You've already answered your own question, and if you put that amazing truth in the very middle of your heart and life, your confidence will grow. Christmas celebrates the incarnation of Christ so that he could be fully human to live a perfect life for us in our place as our Substitute. He also offered that pure and sinless body as a sin offering—*but he never stopped being God*! He wasn't a little bit divine, or half and half—he was still the all-powerful Son of the Most High, Co-Creator of the universe. Think about that for just a minute—it was the *blood of God* that was drawn by the lash, the thorns, the nails, and spear!

If Jesus were just one human being, his perfect life and

death would help only him. Because he is man and God, his blood is powerful enough and universal enough and timeless enough to wash all the people of the world. Is that a staggering and even unbelievable concept? Yes. But believe it anyway, not because I said it but because God said it: **"Look, the Lamb of God, who takes away the sin of the world!"** (John 1:29).

God's love is universal. **"God so loved *the world* that he gave his one and only Son, that whoever believes in him shall not perish but have eternal life"** (John 3:16). Your faith now connects you with his magnificent grace. As big as your pile of sins may be, as big as a pile of all the sand on Miami Beach, Christ's forgiveness is bigger still. His Word says so.

● ● ● ● ● ● ●

Q: I have a sister who is mentally disabled and has been all her life. I work in a group home with adults who have mental and physical disabilities. My question and concern is are they okay with God? They don't understand. Some just like my sister don't talk, and the level of their understanding is of a very young child. I know that we are all born in sin. What happens when they can't understand this or even know who Jesus is?

A: What wonderful life work you have chosen! May God bless your every effort to love and assist these dear people.

Alas, your sister inherited the same sinful flesh you did from your sinful father and sinful mother. She needs a Savior just as much as you do. Sinfulness is not just a matter of *doing* evil—it's *being* evil. It's in our bones and flesh, as Jesus showed Nicodemus. But the same Savior whose blood has washed you clean has washed her too. And the same Holy

Spirit who accomplished the miracle of conversion in you is capable of converting her, creating saving faith in her heart, and indwelling her as he does you.

Jesus' disciples struggled with that concept. They tried to shoo little children away from Jesus, since they thought that children's little minds couldn't grasp the things Jesus was saying. Jesus rebuked them: **"Truly I tell you, anyone who will not receive the kingdom of God like a little child will never enter it"** (Mark 10:15). In other words, not only can little children believe in God too, their simple, miraculous faith is a paradigm and model for us all.

All faith is created by God. It has nothing to do with our own brilliance or size of vocabulary. In fact, the smarter we are the more Satan has a field day with throwing up one objection after another. The more you think you know about the universe, the easier it is for Satan to get his hooks into you.

Was your sister baptized? She may never intellectually be able to grasp or articulate Baptism's meaning. But she can benefit from it because Baptism is 100 percent God's work. It is a legacy gift, just as if she had received a bequest from a relative. If little children can receive the kingdom through the powerful work of the Spirit, she can too. (If she hasn't been baptized, please see to that ASAP, okay?)

8

"I will come back and take you to be with me that you also may be where I am. You know the way to the place where I am going" (John 14:4).

Hell, Death, and Heaven

Q: Is hell an actual, physical place or as one pastor contends, a state of being?

A: In a sense hell has two stages. Hell right now is a place where the *spirits* of the disobedient and unbelievers are imprisoned (see 1 Peter 3:19). Their judgment has been pronounced and their eternal destiny is fixed. Their spirit torment has begun, even as their bodies are still in their graves. Could that be called a "state of being"? It certainly is a miserable state of being. The endless self-loathing, bitterness, hatred, blaming, self-pity, and regrets are just beginning.

On the great day of judgment, all spirits of the deceased will receive their bodies back and their eternal judgment will be made public. **"Multitudes who sleep in the dust of the earth will awake: some to everlasting life, others to shame and everlasting contempt"** (Daniel 12:2). For the damned, this ushers in Stage 2 of hell. Now they will suffer body *and* soul.

Will this stage of hell be a *place*? Jesus described it so in his parable of the rich man and Lazarus. The rich man in hell pleads, **"I beg you, father, send Lazarus to my family, for I have five brothers. Let him warn them, so that they will not also come to this *place* of torment"** (Luke 16:27,28). According to Jesus, not even a drop of water will be available to ease their suffering.

The Bible describes hell both as a state of punishment (Matthew 25:46) and separation from God: **"They will be punished with everlasting destruction and shut out from the presence of the Lord and from the glory of his might"** (2 Thessalonians 1:9). Scripture does not tell us where this place will be, except to assure us that **"a great chasm has been set in place,"** between heaven and hell, so that it will be impossible to cross over (Luke 16:26).

This horrible coming reality lends urgency to the Christians' mission on this earth in the here and now. We must tell people of the Savior who suffered hell on a cross so that we wouldn't have to. **"There is now no condemnation for those who are in Christ Jesus"** (Romans 8:1).

● ● ● ● ● ● ●

Q: Did all the people who died before Jesus came go to hell?

A: No way.

All people of all time have the same way to receive God's mercy and forgiveness, live a fulfilling and joyful life, and spend eternity in heaven—it comes only through faith in Jesus. The people before his day could believe God's promises of the Messiah who *would come* just as we believe God's words about the Messiah who *did come*. God's earliest revelations of his Word, all the way back to the Garden of Eden, contained those precious promises.

Jesus taught that the Old Testament was really all

about him! He once said, **"You study the** [Old Testament]
**Scriptures diligently because you think that in them
you have eternal life. These are the very Scriptures that
testify about me"** (John 5:39). After describing the crucially
important events of Good Friday, Easter, and Pentecost,
Peter told a crowd at the temple, **"Indeed, beginning with
Samuel, all the prophets who have spoken have foretold
these days"** (Acts 3:24).

Jesus' incredible work for our salvation generated a huge
tidal wave of his forgiving blood. It spread horizontally,
covering everyone in the world at his time, and it spread
vertically in both directions, both pouring forward till the
end of time and gushing backward all the way to Adam
and Eve.

Give me some examples of Old Testament believers who
are in heaven, you say? Well, how about:

- King David. He closes Psalm 17 in this way: **"As for
me, I will be vindicated and will see your face; when
I awake, I will be satisfied with seeing your likeness"**
(verse 15).

- Abraham. Jesus' parable of the rich man and Lazarus
reveals Abraham at God's right hand.

- The sons of Korah (a musicians' guild). Psalm 49:15 has
this confident statement: **"God will redeem me from
the realm of the dead; he will surely take me
to himself."**

- Moses and Elijah, who came down from heaven to join
Jesus on the Mount of Transfiguration (Matthew 17:1-13).

- The great catalog of Old Testament heroes in Hebrews
chapter 11. The chapter concludes: **"These were all**

commended for their faith, yet none of them received what had been promised, since God had planned something better for us so that only together with us would they be made perfect" (11:39,40).

● ● ● ● ● ● ●

Q: I watched one of your programs on anger. You said Cain is currently suffering in hell. My question is, Where in the Bible is it said that once an unrepentant sinner dies, he/she goes to burn in hell for eternity?

A: First, a quick comment on Cain. Even his wretched sins of hatred and murder were not his most serious problem. Cain essentially was an unbeliever going through some of the motions of a believer. First John 3:12 tells us that Cain belonged to the evil one. The holy writer Jude calls down God's wrath on evildoers who **"have taken the way of Cain"** (Jude 1:11).

Scripture teaches that God intends hell to be a place of *permanent* judgment and torment for all those who are not connected to their Savior Jesus Christ. Here are a few examples: **"The worms that eat them *will not die*, the fire that burns them *will not be quenched*, and they will be loathsome to all mankind"** (Isaiah 66:24). **"The smoke of their torment will rise *for ever and ever*"** (Revelation 14:11). **"Then they** [the condemned] **will go away to *eternal punishment*, but the righteous to eternal life"** (Matthew 25:46). Jesus' point: hell lasts as long as heaven.

Perhaps you have heard the objections from people who think an eternal hell is too severe to expect from a God who is supposed to be merciful. Actually both concepts are true. God's mercy is far greater than anything you could imagine. There is no parallel on earth to the greatness of the Father's love that would sacrifice his own Son for the sins of the world. But there is also no parallel on earth for God's wrath—it is worse than anything you could imagine. **"The smoke of their torment will rise for ever."**

Tell people the truth. You're just the messenger. People should be afraid of hell. They need to embrace Jesus Christ in faith. Now.

* * * * * * *

Q: If I were to die while smoking or drinking, would I go to hell even though I believe in Jesus?

A: I have to answer this one in layers. First, be careful of judging others, or yourself, in regard to tobacco and alcohol consumption. There is nothing at all in the Bible about tobacco, and drinking of alcohol was most certainly not forbidden in either the Old or New Testament. Our Lord Jesus created a huge quantity of wine at the wedding at Cana, his very first miracle. He chose bread and wine to be the earthly elements in his heavenly meal—the Lord's Supper. Neither tobacco use nor alcohol use *in and of themselves* is sinful.

I hasten to add that the Bible emphatically condemns drunkenness. It also urges us to see our bodies as temples of the Holy Spirit, and so we should avoid activities that harm or damage them. Everyone who chooses to use tobacco should beware of its power to addict and poison. Nicotine is one of the most powerful of drugs. Heavy daily use puts a tar coating on the fragile tissue of the lungs.

The essence of your question is not drinking or smoking, but the presence of *any* sin in the last moments of your life. Remember this: you are saved by your faith in Christ, not by what you have done or not done. Our faith does not die every time we sin. We will be sinners until the day we die. We aren't falling in and out of grace each day; we don't have to live in terror that our death or judgment day will catch us in a down cycle. Repent each day of the sins of which you are aware, give to Jesus all those you can't remember or didn't notice, welcome his gospel forgiveness, and live for him with all your heart. Tomorrow repeat the cycle.

● ● ● ● ● ● ●

Q: If someone we love commits suicide, does he or she automatically go to hell? I wonder if they were sick enough to do this to themselves, would God forgive them? Isn't it just like drug users who keep using drugs even though they know they will die?

A: The sad, sad circumstances of suicide will always carry the dreadful shadow of the suicide of Judas. After betraying Jesus, Judas had a fit of remorse and tried to give the betrayal money back to his "employers." They wouldn't take it. Judas threw the money in the temple and then went out and committed suicide by hanging himself (Matthew 27:5). The evangelist Luke comments grimly that Judas **"left to go where he belongs,"** i.e., hell (Acts 1:25).

We should be very careful of putting the story of Judas onto the desperate and miserable people who commit suicide. Suicide is a terrible sin—the murder of self is still murder, and because it ends a person's life, it doesn't leave the individual with time to reflect and repent. Still, it's not that the sin of suicide is too big for Jesus to forgive. He shed the blood of God himself on the cross! It is bigger than any wrong we could ever do.

What matters is if the person still believes in Christ, however weakly. A weak faith in a strong Savior still brings the holiness before God that we need when we stand before the judgment. It is possible that a person who commits suicide has abandoned whatever faith he or she might have had. Or—it is possible that the person suffered from some mental illness or delusions and acted in an impulsive fit of despair *but still had some measure of faith in his or her heart.*

I presided at the funeral of a man who killed himself, but I had heard so many sincere expressions of his faith that I am convinced that he acted out of weakness of faith, not absence of faith. I would suggest that unless the deceased exhibited open contempt for God, we draw the veil of charity and give the person the benefit of the doubt. After all, we are not that person's judge—God is. Let's let God do his business—he always gets it right.

As we march along on life's journey, let's be aware that many of the people around us are absolutely miserable in their lives. They are trying to put on a brave face, but their despair closes over them like heavy darkness. Let's take people's suicide talk seriously—people say those things because they are reaching out for help. It costs us so little to say words of encouragement and praise. If you yourself feel the despair of severe depression, don't be afraid to ask for help. God answers our cries by sending people into our lives. Let them in. Let's invest energy in the fellowship of our congregations and take care of each other.

* * * * * * *

Q: In today's world, I hear people talking about heaven as if it's a place where nice people go when they die. I don't think they're talking about the heaven of the Bible. If you are a good person but don't believe in Jesus, are you still going to hell?

A: It all depends on who is defining what a "nice" person is.

People are very willing to provide their own definitions. Usually they set the bar pretty low (probably to make sure that they can jump over it too). You know, I have never attended a funeral where the pastor said, "Well, this is a sad day. Bob's in hell now." Nope. Every funeral preacher puts a shine on the memory of the deceased and tries to give the funeral attendees an obituary that leaves the bereaved with some degree of comfort and pride.

We all know "nice" people. They cut their grass, pay their taxes, and don't throw garbage on your lawn. They are decent citizens. Their neighbors and relatives think they are nice people. Neighbors and friends can award prizes at the neighborhood block party in summer, but they will not determine where the individual will spend eternity.

The only one whose opinion of the deceased matters at all is God. There is no fooling him. He can see right through people. He knows when he is being played. He knows who's faking it. If you have a lot of friends who think you are a nice person but you have no faith in Christ, you will die in your sins. God will not call you nice. Hell awaits all those without a Savior. They may even think they were "spiritual" people. But unless you are connected to Christ by faith, you are a faker. **"Many will say to me on that day, 'Lord, Lord.' . . . Then I will tell them plainly, 'I never knew you. Away from me, you evildoers!'"** (Matthew 7:22-24). Sin is a poisonous disease from hell, and no human being can come up with the antidote.

It is Jesus Christ who has crushed the head of the serpent, as God foretold to Eve in Genesis 3:15. He alone paid our debts. He alone is the Way, the Truth, and the Life. No one is acceptable to God except through him (John 14:6). Here are those whom God considers nice, those who *believe* these words: **"But he** [Christ] **has appeared once for all at the culmination of the ages to do away with sin by the sacrifice of himself. Just as people are destined to die once, and after that to face judgment, so Christ was sacrificed once to take away the sins of many; and he will appear a second time, not to bear sin, but to bring salvation to those who are waiting for him"** (Hebrews 9:26-28).

If you die without Christ, you have nothing. If you have nothing on earth but die with Christ, you have everything. Everything that matters.

* * * * * * *

Q: Where in the Bible does it say that we will go to heaven?

A: Let me encourage you to grab your Bible today and sit down with the last two chapters of the Bible. After telling the story of the warfare that God's people will have to endure and overcome, Christ's ultimate triumph over Satan and his demons is foretold. And then the curtains open on the beautiful and peaceful vision of what awaits us. Read 'em both. Slowly. And then go back and read 'em again. You will never be the same.

Here is what the end of human history on this earth will look like: **"For the Lord himself will come down from heaven, with a loud command, with the voice of the archangel and with the trumpet call of God, and the dead in Christ will rise first. After that, we who are still alive and are left will be caught up together with them in the clouds to meet the Lord in the air. And so we will be with the Lord forever"** (1 Thessalonians 4:16,17).

The apostle John as an old man was allowed briefly to see the triumphant multitudes who will surround God in worship and adoration: **"After this I looked, and there before me was a great multitude that no one could count, from every nation, tribe, people and language, standing before the throne and before the Lamb. They were wearing white robes and were holding palm branches in their hands. And they cried out in a loud voice: 'Salvation belongs to our God, who sits on the throne, and to the Lamb.' All the angels were standing around the throne and around the elders and the four living creatures. They fell down on their faces before the throne and worshiped God"** (Revelation 7:9–11).

Who gets to go? You know the answer: **"God so loved the world that he gave his one and only Son, that whoever believes in him shall not perish but have eternal life"** (John 3:16).

* * * * * * *

Q: Our souls will be with God, but do we get new bodies in heaven?

A: Yes and yes. Both your statements are true. They refer to different stages of God's unfolding plan.

Stage 1 is what happens when believers die in the here and now. The soul or spirit detaches from the physical body, which slowly begins to return to the dust and dirt that we are made of. The soul rises to God's presence and the experience of heavenly joy. Scripture has many references to the fact that souls or spirits can have memory, identity, personality, individuality, and the ability to communicate. The angels occasionally adopted human "costumes" when they interacted with people in their trips to earth, and so perhaps the spirits of the saints have the temporary semblance of a human body while they wait.

Angel-spirits have the capacity for emotion—they rejoice when sinners repent—so my assumption is that human-spirits experience the joy of God's presence. Finally they are safe. Finally they sin no more. Finally they don't have to suffer the voice of the tempter. They are reunited with all the believers of the past and watch with joy as the heavenly host of saints grows each day.

But then comes judgment day, and the heavenly experience will change. Stage 2 begins. First, the trumpets blast, and earth and sea yield their dead. It doesn't matter how many fragments of people's bodies are left—their DNA is on file in God's heavenly servers, and he can reassemble a body from the dust in a snap. **"Multitudes who sleep in the dust of the earth will awake: some to everlasting life, others to shame and everlasting contempt. Those who are wise will shine like the brightness of the heavens, and those who lead many to righteousness, like the stars for ever and ever"** (Daniel 12:2,3).

Jesus rose from the dead with his body, his real, physical body. He could touch and be touched. He could utter words with a real tongue and chew and eat food (John 21:15). He had real lungs and could breathe (John 20:22). It was really *his* body—the same one crucified for us. The nail marks were still in his hands and feet and the scar from the spear thrust still visible and touchable in his side.

You will get your body back, but not in the condition in which it was buried. You will be 100 percent restored. No more disabilities. No more debilities of aging. Lost limbs restored. All five senses fully operational. Mind refreshed.

All the energy and vitality of youth will return. It will still be the authentic you.

It will be your same old body, but made like new.

• • • • • • •

Q: Are there really "many rooms" in a house in heaven? Is that where we will "live"?

A: You are referring to Jesus' thrilling and encouraging words from the upper room on Maundy Thursday evening. To his gloomy and apprehensive disciples, Jesus gave this comforting prophecy: **"My Father's house has many rooms; if that were not so, would I have told you that I am going there to prepare a place for you? And if I go and prepare a place for you, I will come back and take you to be with me that you also may be where I am"** (John 14:2,3).

The Bible uses many metaphors for what heaven will be like. These linguistic pictures help us wrap our heads around an experience that is beyond human language, so don't press the literal details. Heaven won't be a literal constructed building, like a ginormous resort hotel, at which all of the hundreds of millions of believers from all ages will be housed. Jesus' point is simply that there will be plenty of room for everybody, and you will rejoice to be home.

Scripture has other beautiful and comforting metaphors to describe the indescribable:

• A city, the new Jerusalem

• A garden, the Paradise of the blessed

• A sumptuous banquet hall

• A glorious temple

· A royal palace with the elegant throne of the Ancient of Days at the center

Heaven is all of these things and much more, more than your senses can handle. It will be totally worth the wait, worth the struggle, worth enduring whatever you have to endure. And yes, that is where we will live.

That is where we will come alive!

* * * * * * *

Q: Do you believe that when we die the loved ones who died before us will know us in heaven?

A: I do indeed. In Jesus' parable of the rich man and Lazarus (Luke 16:19–31), the rich man in hell readily indentified Abraham in heaven. On the Mount of Transfiguration, Jesus not only recognized Moses and Elijah coming back to earth but had an earnest conversation with both of them (Luke 9:28–33).

When miraculous resurrections took place during the ministry of Christ and the apostles, the people who were raised recognized the people in their former lives. **"Women received back their dead, raised to life again"** (Hebrews 11:35). Jesus once instructed believers to be generous with their wealth and invest in people: **"I tell you, use worldly wealth to gain friends for yourselves, so that when it is gone, you will be welcomed into eternal dwellings"** (Luke 16:9). The obvious assumption: those people who got to heaven first will recognize you when you arrive and thank you.

You will be you in heaven, not somebody else. You will look like yourself—not the way you looked the moment you died, but the way you were designed to look in your prime.

You will have your identity and at least most (or maybe even all) of your memories, for it is our memories that give us our personality. The souls of the martyrs waiting for judgment day had certainly not lost their memories of things that had happened during their earthly lives (Revelation 6:10).

Heaven will be not just a thrilling escape from death and Satan. It will be the beginning of the Grand Reunion.

* * * * * * *

Q: If the devil was able to sin, how do I know that sin won't creep into heaven like it did the Garden of Eden?

A: What the grand sweep of the Bible's narrative lays out for us is that God built a time of testing for both people and angels. The majority of the holy angels passed their test, and they are now confirmed and immovable in their holiness. The demons who rebelled are now confirmed in their hellish destiny. They will not have access to tempt and torment the saints in heaven because they and their devilish master are going headfirst into the lake of burning sulfur (Revelation 20:10). In heaven we will live in complete safety and serenity.

Like the good angels, the saints will be confirmed in their holiness too. **"The trumpet will sound, the dead will be raised *imperishable*, and we will be changed"** (1 Corinthians 15:52). The Greek word used for our resurrected bodies means "incorruptible." The time of testing is over. Heaven and earth are now identical—the new earth will be heaven. Heaven won't be on earth; it will be the earth: **"I heard a loud voice from the throne saying, 'Look! God's dwelling place is now among the people, and he will dwell with them. They will be his people, and God himself** will be with them and be their God. **"He will wipe every tear from their eyes. There will be no more death" or mourning or crying or pain, for the old order of things has passed away'"** (Revelation 21:3,4).

There can't be even the possibility of sin anymore, because sinners always die. God solemnly declares that there will be no death in heaven, so therefore there can't be sin either. **"Nothing impure will ever enter it"** (Revelation 21:27). Sin causes mourning, crying, and pain, and those things are abolished too. I don't know which excites me more—never again to be hurt or that never again will I hurt anyone else.

The greatness of the work of Christ is that he not merely brought us back to the original starting point of the Garden of Eden, where we will have to undergo testing all over again. He brought us to the finish line in Paradise.

* * * * * * *

Q: I'm on my second marriage. Will I be with my first wife or my second wife or neither when I'm in heaven?

A: Normally I wouldn't venture out into that live fire zone with my own speculations. But Jesus himself once heard a question similar to that, and he answered it by revealing that in heaven **"they will neither marry nor be given in marriage; they will be like the angels"** (Mark 12:25).

What he means by that is we will not be bonded to one spouse for all eternity. There won't be any fighting over who "gets" whom if one of the believers was married multiple times on earth and one or more spouses is in heaven too. That doesn't mean, though, that you will be unaware of the people who have great significance to you on this earth. It doesn't mean that you will not be able to live in close proximity or enjoy really strong relationships with people that will continue on into heaven. It just won't be with the earthly rules for marriage.

Just what that type of relationship will be—I don't think God can trust us with that information yet. It will be revealed to us at the right time. If you are worrying about those things right now, relax—it's all going to work out. We will enjoy *all* our relationships from this earth, and God will figure out a way in which we won't be sort of fighting for exclusive rights over other people. We will be able to enjoy our wonderful spiritual family in heaven to the full.

* * * * * * *

Q: Can you tell me what words of encouragement I might find to help me through the pain of losing my dog? Are there specific passages that refer to our animals? Will we see them again in heaven?

A: Ah, what a tender question. Our pets are more than animals, aren't they? They are friends, companions, and partners in life's adventures. Their emotions seem so human—how they burrow into our hearts!

God cares about his animal creatures, including your dog. Jesus taught a large crowd once just how valuable they were to God: **"Are not two sparrows sold for a penny? Yet not one of them will fall to the ground outside your Father's care"** (Matthew 10:29). He cares about them in general and pays attention to each one specifically! God notices *each* duck, goldfish, cat, bear, dog, giraffe, hamster, moose, and elephant, providing food and habitat appropriate for each.

Christians have been wrestling with the question about

animals in heaven for centuries. Catholics look to 13th century St. Francis of Assisi for inspiration. According to legend, he once preached to the birds, who flocked around him and were not afraid of him. Statuary and paintings of the famous saint often show him with a bird, and some Catholic churches on his feast day will feature the blessing of people's pets.

Protestant pet lovers have their own authority. Martin Luther himself loved dogs and had one that he named *Toelpel* ("numskull"). When his daughter was grieving over the dog's death, he assured her that she would see him again in heaven, for in God's perfect world he would not deny her that happiness. One of Luther's many houseguests claimed to have heard him remark to the dog once, "Be comforted, little dog. You, too, in the Resurrection shall have a little golden tail."

I think it's great fun to quote famous people and bat around personal opinions. But we should observe a little humility around too-confident predictions of what God is going to do in the new heavens and new earth. Scripture does tell us that we will rise with our bodies and live in a physical universe. Hosea 2:18 tells us that in God's new world the animals will no longer be a threat to people **"so that all may lie down in safety."** Since the Bible describes heaven as containing vegetation, I expect plants. The way God has designed plants actually requires animal interaction for certain things like pollination, isn't it so? Thus it seems logical to guess that there will be animals in heaven to complete the ecosystem.

I personally expect to see them. But—will I meet Rebel, my family's miniature schnauzer, again? Will there be a grand resurrection of *specific* animals? Will there be a great separation of believing and unbelieving pets on judgment day? Will bad dogs go to hell? *Hmm.*

Let's just wait and see. God's surprises in heaven will astound and delight us.

● ● ● ● ● ● ●

Q: Where are we after we die but before the Last Day when we rise again as Jesus promised?

A: I think every believer has wondered about those things at one time or another. The Lord has not yet revealed the full story of the things that will be happening after we die, but he has given us some clues.

Here's what we know from Scripture: Your body literally dies and goes back to the earth from which it was made, ashes to ashes and dust to dust. But God will have absolutely no trouble putting it back together. In fact, 1 Corinthians 15:52 says that he will reassemble you **"in a flash, in the twinkling of an eye, at the last trumpet."**

Even while we are waiting for that mighty trumpet sound, though, the souls or spirits of those who have died do live on. There are a number of fascinating examples in the Scriptures to show that consciousness does continue and that in your soul or spirit you in effect have a private judgment day. When you die you go either to hell or heaven *in spirit.* For the hell component, just think of what happened to the Lord Jesus himself. First Peter chapter 3 says that even before walking out of the tomb on Easter Sunday morning, Jesus went in spirit to the nether regions of hell. There he proclaimed his great triumph to the souls and spirits of the disobedient who now live there permanently. Presumably Satan and the demons could hear their bad news too.

Scripture also has a fascinating peek into the world of the

blessed souls in heaven who are eagerly waiting for judgment day, waiting both for justice and the Grand Reunion. Revelation 6:9,10 states, **"I saw under the altar the souls of those who had been slain because of the word of God and the testimony they had maintained. They called out in a loud voice, 'How long, Sovereign Lord, holy and true, until you judge the inhabitants of the earth and avenge our blood?'"** This passage clearly shows that the souls of the saints have alertness, consciousness, and the ability to communicate with God already in heaven *before judgment day.*

* * * * * * *

Q: Will I be saved and go to heaven if I do not go to the church or belong to the faith that my parents brought me up in?

A: That's a question that a lot of families have to deal with. It seems as if there are many, many Christians today who have chosen a different path of faith, a different denomination, a different "brand" of Christianity, from that of their parents. The National Association of Evangelicals reports that 60 percent of evangelical Christian leaders have changed denominations. Now when Christians leave the church body of their youth to join another, that may cause some heartburn with their parents. But does God care?

First of all, what matters here is not my opinion or even your opinion. What matters is what God says. To answer the question, Where is my everlasting destiny? Am I going to be saved or not? go to the one place where you can have absolute confidence in the answers and the information—the Bible. There is nothing in the Bible that says you are obligated as a condition of your salvation to stay in the religious organization into which you happen to be born. If it works for you, if you believe it and embrace it, if you have confidence in its biblical integrity, if there is a branch of that faith where you're living currently and you can continue in it, there's enormous benefit in that.

What really matters is not so much your membership loyalty to the organization in which you grew up; what really matters is the degree to which the organization where you choose to belong now is loyal to the Word of God. What really matters is if you believe and recognize from Scripture that you are a sinner who desperately needs God's mercy by birth, a sinner in need of saving. Do you believe that Jesus Christ was born and lived for you and that his death and resurrection bring you the forgiveness and immortality that you need? Does your current pastor have a rock-solid commitment to teaching the Scriptures?

What will ease the conversations with your parents is the assurance that though you might have left the denomination of your youth, you have not left the common faith and beliefs you know to be true from the Word.

● ● ● ● ● ● ●

Q: If God can truly do anything and is really who you say he is, why would he let my nine-month-old daughter die? I can't imagine a good God letting something like that happen.

A: What a painful question, a very personal question. First of all, let's establish the first part of what you ask—is God really unlimited in his power? Is God really unlimited in his love for us, and does he really have the intellect and brains to manage the universe? And the answers are yes, yes, and yes. You truly can have absolute trust in God's power, his wisdom, and his love. All are *guaranteed* to you in the cross of Christ.

Then comes the question: Why would he allow a disaster like this to come slamming into a family? My short answer: I don't know in this specific case why God would allow this to happen. For that matter, why would God allow any evil to happen to his children?

- An automobile accident that causes a disability in one of his believers.

- Believers being laid off from their jobs, causing loss of income that the family badly needs.

- A child is born to believers with birth defects so severe she will need lifetime care by others.

- There's a premature death in a believing family.

What I can tell you is this: you and I as sinners, as people who have consciously rebelled against God's will and ways, have joined Adam and Eve's original rebellion in which they recklessly invited evil and death into our world to stalk us all. Grim Death like a reaper goes after us, and his nasty scythe lands on people of all different ages, including children. Death on earth was not God's design or wish. It is the inevitable consequence of Adam and Eve's rebellion, and their children have been weeping ever since. In fact, I think God is grieving your daughter's death even more than you are.

God's solution to this dilemma was to send his Son, Jesus. The Son's mission was nothing less than the defeat of humanity's greatest enemies: sin, sickness, pain, death, hell, and Satan. He became human and suffered an early death himself in order to buy us the forgiveness of our sins for now and forever. Sin is now forgiven. Death for believers is temporary. Satan's power over us is gone. And we will never see hell.

Even a little one like your daughter who is nine months old can receive the washing of Holy Baptism, God's gift of the forgiveness of sins, and the promise of immortality. She isn't lost to you forever. She is safe and waiting for you. We'll see her soon. Would you introduce me when we do?

* * * * * * * *

Q: Why does God choose to heal some people, yet others die?

A: I doubt if there is a believer anywhere who has not wondered about the discrepancies and inequalities in human life. People have wildly different health histories, don't they? But they also have wildly differing amounts of wealth, education, and intelligence. Some have to live through the trauma of war and social upheaval while others live their whole lives with good and peaceful government. Some couples seem to be able to produce babies at will while others bear the pain of infertility.

The truth is, every believer in Christ will indeed experience full and total physical restoration to perfect health—in heaven. Remember that God's ultimate agenda is not to *restore* the earth to the Garden of Eden but to *replace* it. His ultimate goal for you is not to give you heaven on earth now but to get you, faith intact, to his new heaven and new earth.

The prophet Isaiah gives you a peek at that joyful human restoration: **"Then will the eyes of the blind be opened and the ears of the deaf unstopped. Then will the lame leap like** a deer, and the mute tongue shout for joy" (Isaiah 35:5,6).

In the meantime we will continue to live in a topsy-turvy world. Your life will probably involve many ups and downs, as did St. Paul's life, who said that he knew what it was like to be in need and to have plenty (Philippians 4:12). God blessed him both in hardship and prosperity, and he uses us for his wonderful agenda in both sickness and health.

What we can celebrate is that our illnesses are not punishments. All the punishing has already been done to Christ on his cross. God allows us to encounter hardships **"so that the works of God might be displayed in him"** (John 9:3). He loves to bless us and restore our failing bodies to health. He has many good things to give us and waits to be asked. But we will have to leave it to his discernment when it fits his agenda best not to provide a miraculous healing. We joyfully await our full restoration in heaven.

● ● ● ● ● ● ●

Q: Do aborted babies go to heaven?

A: I don't know. I am comforted in my ignorance that nobody else does either. I also need to keep my mouth shut on the destiny of partially formed children in the womb who died of miscarriage or stillbirth. Scripture simply does not speak directly to these two issues, and so neither should we.

It would be nice if we could say that people who have died as victims of violence automatically go to heaven. We don't know that. It would be nice if we could assure grieving parents that children of Christian parents who have died before birth were guaranteed heaven because of parental faith in Christ. We have no scriptural basis to say that. It would be nice if we could assure people that prayer can convert the unborn, but there is no Word of God to establish that idea either.

The only ways God has given us to share salvation with people are the means of grace—the Word and the washing of Baptism. Neither of those can be applied to the unborn. They can't hear or understand speech, and the water of Baptism cannot touch their little bodies, so we have to wait till they're born. In the case of the unborn who lose their lives before birth, they are out of our reach. Thus their destinies belong to God alone.

The unborn are people too. King David praised God for carefully fashioning his tiny body in the womb (Psalm 139:13-16). John the Baptist leaped for joy in the presence of the Savior even before he or Jesus was born (Luke 1:41). Each of these little ones already has a fully developed set of DNA, the genetic code that contains the blueprints for a fully-formed adult. Sad to say, the unborn have already inherited their sinful flesh from their parents. David realized that his sinful inclinations could be traced all the way back to the time his mother conceived him (Psalm 51:5).

We can be comforted in the knowledge that God's decisions on the destinies of these little ones will be just right. There will be perfect justice for each one. While God does not allow us to offer salvation except through the means of grace, he can make his own exceptions.

* * * * * * *

Q: My husband recently died of brain cancer, and I just don't understand why God took him to heaven *now*? I know we're not supposed to understand God's long-term plans for us. Did God take him home since his work on this earth was completed? What Scripture can I read that will get me through and give me comfort?

A: Even though you know he's safe with the Lord, even though you want to let go and let God, you still can't accept it. I resonate with your pain right now. I wish I knew for sure the right answers to your questions, but I don't.

There are just so many divine possibilities. Did your husband take ill and die because God made an executive decision to end his life? Could have happened that way. But it's more likely that God's heart was grieved by your husband's illness and merely *allowed* it. Big difference. Not everything that happens in life is by God's direct intervention. Some things he *lets happen* because the human race long ago chose to live in a broken world. God created a world without sin and death. Now he comes to help and patch things together to keep us going and ultimately to restore us. His answer to human suffering and death was to send his Son, Jesus, to experience suffering and death, all so he could give us our lives back.

One thing I know for sure is that God's ultimate mission in our lives is to draw us closer to him and make our faith strong. Sometimes he does that by blessing us. Sometimes he makes our hardships and sufferings do the same thing. Another thing I know is that God will help and sustain you in some ways you don't yet see. He will also use this passing to advance his agenda, also in ways you probably can't yet see. None of your struggle and heart hurt will be wasted.

I leave you with a thought, a personal belief of mine, that I don't remember ever hearing or reading from someone else. Jesus told us that in heaven we will neither marry nor be given in marriage (Matthew 22:30). That is a sad thought to widows whose only desire is to be reunited with their husbands. Well . . . maybe in heaven we can be trusted to live together without marriage? That doesn't work on earth because of our sinful inclinations, but in heaven? I can't think of any reason why you and your late husband couldn't choose to find one another in heaven's world and join your lives together as much as possible. Thus your separation would be only temporary.

In the meantime, God will send kind people into your life and cause things to happen that will soften the blow and give you joy to sustain you. Your personal suffering will even more fully equip you to bear witness to the hope of forgiveness and everlasting life that we have only through Jesus. Come soon, Lord Jesus!

9

*"Go into all the world and preach the
gospel to all creation" (Mark 16:15).*

Telling Others the Good News

Q: How do I know that God wants me to be part of his
rescue team? I don't really feel worthy of it.

A: You know, if we all needed to be worthy of everything
that God wanted to use us for, nobody would ever do
anything for the Lord. The prophet Amos was a sycamore-fig
tree tender minding his own business when the Lord called.
Moses thought that he was way too tongue-tied to represent
the Lord God of Israel. Jeremiah thought he was just a child,
too insignificant to expect anyone to pay attention to him.

We're all sinners. We've all fallen short of the glory of
God. We're all in need of his mercy. But that painful reality
in and of itself is what makes this all work. When God has
awakened within us a sense of our own unworthiness, then
he can fill us up with his mercy—pronouncing us to be not
guilty of our sins, loving us unlovely people, and making
us feel like we're worth something. It is *his* power that
transforms us so we can rise above ourselves. He makes
us better than we are. It is *his* message that comes out of
our mouths, not our own reasonings, experiences, and
personal philosophies.

One of the great ironies of the way in which God gets his

work done is that some of the most powerful testimonies come from people who are broken, who have failed in their past, who are not the high and mighty but rather the small and low.

To join God's rescue team simply means that you are going to do for somebody else what someone else has done for you. You help that person see how good God is:

- How eager he is to be reunited with his lost children.

- How powerful his Spirit is to change our insides.

- How wonderful it is to have Jesus Christ's daily mercy coming to us. His grace really is new every morning.

- How reassuring it is never again to be afraid to die.

- How joyful it is to have a reason to be glad to be alive, a reason to be confident of our relationship with God, and a reason to show that same mercy and kindness to other people and make God look good to them.

● ● ● ● ● ● ●

Q: If God already predetermined who will be saved, what is the point of witnessing?

A: There are two "time realities" in existence. You and I are on the train car called The Present. We are a moving dot, with the past behind us and the unknown future ahead of us. God on the other hand is above and beyond time. He can see everything that has happened and everything that will happen as easily as he can see what's happening right now. We can get ourselves twisted up in philosophical knots by trying to answer questions from both realities at the same time.

The Bible describes God as interacting with humanity in

both "time realities." Sometimes he arranges things from all eternity; sometimes he gets involved in our "present" and adjusts his course of action according to how people think, talk, and act. They are both true simultaneously, and we will never be able to determine with 100 percent accuracy which are the direct causes of things that happen. Sometimes events have multiple causes. Was I brought to faith because of God's divine choosing or because someone in my family taught me about Jesus? The answer is yes.

The Bible tells us about God's eternal foreknowledge and predestination for only one reason—so that you give him all the glory and praise for your saving faith. That's it. Don't try to dig into God's mind and guess at the *why*. The Bible assigns only one cause if a person is condemned on the Day of Judgment and ends up in hell. It is the person's own unbelief and rejection of the Word.

God doesn't want us to know his predestination choices. He wants us to view *all* the people of the world as objects of his mercy and tell the gospel story. God will indeed get all the chosen ones home, but in the meantime you and I are God's instruments of salvation. He has no other plan. The Bible does not self-proclaim. The Word needs to be set in motion by believers in order to have its power touch the hearts and minds of the people around us.

Since we don't know who the chosen are, *we need to tell them all.*

* * * * * * *

Q: How long do you think you should know people before you start evangelizing to them?

A: You will never know for sure what's going on in people's

minds or where they are on their spiritual journey, so just use your best judgment. Gauge where your relationship is. I have two suggestions. First, if your relationship is kind of casual and light, maybe the best way to start is to ask that person to come with you to experience the Word together, to go to some kind of Christian event, to hear some Christian music, attend a home Bible study, or to go to a concert with you. Maybe he or she would be your guest and join you at a worship service. Invite them to come along as your guests and sit with them. Try to keep your opinions to yourself and later let them express what they thought of the experience.

When your relationship has progressed to the point where you know each other fairly well and there's a degree of trust, how do you broach the subject of explaining God's work of salvation? The first imperative is always to listen first. Ask a lot of questions and draw out where people are at. Don't assume you know where their beliefs are, and you don't want to make them feel that you are "preaching" at them. You will want to know what beliefs you already have in common and where the gaps are in their understanding. Listening and questions show respect.

Second, don't get too fancy or try to be somebody you're not. Just tell people what God has done. You don't have to try to argue with people; you don't have to give a comprehensive overview of all of Christian doctrine; you don't have to try to crush every one of their false ideas. Just say what God has done: That our Lord Jesus loves you so much that he came to offer his life to be able to give you the forgiveness of your sins, joy and peace in your everyday life, and the wonderful hope of immortality.

• • • • • • • •

Q: I want to invite a friend to church who has previously said no several times. Can you give me some advice?

A: I love the fact that you said "invite." I think if you say to somebody, "You know, you *ought* to do this or that," "You *ought* to go to church," you probably won't have very much success. Perhaps the person knows that already but just doesn't like to get pushed around. Pulling is always more likely to succeed than pushing.

What have you learned about the person's prior refusals? Did you ask? Do you think you know why? Were you patient enough and inquisitive enough and nonjudgmental enough for the person to tell you the truth about his reluctance? Was the real answer a hard "no" or a "maybe"?

Perhaps your friend has had some bad experiences with Christians or a Christian church in the past. Are you comfortable enough with your own faith to let your friend pour out some bitterness without jumping all over him?

Perhaps you could start more indirectly by giving him a devotional booklet or watching a Christian television program together (smile). You can share Christian materials or links via e-mail in little doses so that he can process them at his own speed.

Friends do things for friends. Are you willing to do something of your friend's choosing just because? Perhaps he would reciprocate: "It would mean a lot to me if we would go together." "Would you come with me, and then we can go out for brunch?" "Would you come with me? I would like to spend some time with you, and I'd like you to know a little bit about my world and my life and something very important to me." Couch it in terms of an adventure that the two of you can do together.

Let it be understood that you are not trying to push the other person around and that you actually would really like to hear his reaction to what he saw and heard.

● ● ● ● ● ● ●

Q: How do I share biblical truths, such as Jesus' "I Am" metaphors, that are hard to understand even for strong Christians?

A: There are three questions in that one question; let's unpack them one at a time. First, I don't think the metaphors really hurt your message at all. In fact, I think Jesus' metaphors are really helpful. They're picture language, and people, especially those who have not done a lot of deep Bible reading, probably respond better to pictures than to abstract biblical doctrine. So don't be scared of picture language. Just tell those marvelous stories and point out one or two conclusions that you have figured out.

Second, don't put too much pressure on yourself to bring about a great depth of understanding. What God has revealed to us, and we then in turn can reveal to others, is not primarily to *understand* but to *believe*. There are some central features of God—like the Trinity, like Jesus Christ's being simultaneously divine and human—that we will never *understand*. God tells us those things so that so that we believe them. The Bible's pictures build faith.

Third, when you are talking to somebody about an important truth, stay within your own comfort zone and don't try to be somebody else. You don't have to pretend to be a televangelist; you don't have to pretend to be your pastor or a theology professor. Just be yourself and tell the story in the terms that made sense first to you.

Tell why a particular truth of Scripture is compelling to *you*, how it made a difference in your life, how it helped you live more joyfully and confidently, how it improved your relationships, how it strengthened your faith in God.

* * * * * * *

Q: A lot of people don't believe that Jesus actually rose from the dead. What can I do to help them believe? How can I prove it to them?

A: I think what might get you off the track is your last question. Nothing is ever going to *prove* Jesus' resurrection to the satisfaction of somebody who's determined to be an unbeliever. Even when the risen Jesus himself appeared to his disciples, they didn't believe it at first and Jesus needed to talk them off the ledge and let them know it really was he. Even his enemies, who were the ones who put him to death and witnessed his crucifixion, refused to believe that he was actually alive.

Where that certainty comes from does not come from *proof* because Satan will always find a way to spoil people's confidence. We can't offer legal proof; we can't offer scientific proof. The empty tomb of Christ from the very beginning was explained away as the work of grave robbers. Our certainty comes from the Word of God, and you're either going to believe it when God says it or not.

My counsel would be for you simply to read the Bible's accounts of Jesus' resurrection and then follow it up with a walk-through of St. Paul's magnificent essay on the power and meaning of Easter. Let the Spirit take it from there.

* * * * * * *

Q: I have a friend who is an atheist, but he enjoys a good debate with me about religion. How can I get through to him that God is real?

A: You will never know for sure what other people are really thinking, what they really believe deep in their minds and souls. Always give the Spirit a lot of room and a lot of credit for bringing about changes in people's beliefs. Sometimes those changes are silent; sometimes they're delayed; sometimes their friends never realize the impact their words and Christian actions have.

Some people like to self-describe as atheists, but they are doing it to poke their Christian friends. They want to feel free to criticize hypocrisy and lame thinking, lifestyles at variance with Christian principles, and loveless talk. Let them say those things. Smile and be a good listener. Remember it's not you they seem to be rejecting. Their real issue is with God.

You have two immensely powerful forces working for you. One is that everybody, even an atheist, has a conscience. Even atheists know the feeling and taste of guilt; even atheists know some fear in the back of their minds, "What if I'm wrong?" Perhaps they will never admit it to you as they spar with you to keep from seeming to be pushed around. Don't get upset with them; don't lose your patience; don't stop smiling and listening.

The second powerful force working for you is that the Word of God has enormous power, power enough to batter down the walls of unbelief around a human heart, power enough to cut through skin and muscle right down to the bone and marrow, power to convict the conscience of a hardened rebel, power to change even a persecutor like Paul.

You don't need to put pressure on yourself to win the debates by your skilled debate techniques or superior argumentation or stinging one-liners or witty comebacks. Just tell the truth, and tell how it has changed your life and mind-set. The truth of the gospel will either convert the person or it will not. It's not on you.

● ● ● ● ● ● ●

Q: My daughter stopped going to church, and she doesn't take my grandchildren either. I'm concerned about them, but she shuts me out when I try to talk to her about it. What can I do?

A: I wonder how many Christian families there are in which parents have not worried about one or more or maybe all of their kids? This is a cry from the heart, and it comes from the hearts of many Christian parents. What to do?

1. You cannot believe for somebody else. You can work hard to bring your kids up right, but ultimately they will have to choose the Christian faith for themselves. It does not necessarily make you a failure as a Christian parent any more than it made Jesus a failure to have lost a disciple like Judas. Judas' moral collapse was not from any teaching failures of Christ. Judas chose his path.

2. Sometimes children of Christian parents are working their way through dramas of independence that seem to go on long after their teenage years. Sometimes adult children use this issue as a way to send a message to the parents: "You can't push me around. You can't *make* me." Until they feel that this message has been

delivered, they will choose behaviors that irritate and defy what they perceive is inappropriate pressure from the parents. So—have a tone when you talk to your adult children that shows respect. Ask questions. Listen twice as much as you talk. Control your fear and emotions.

3. Don't give up. Don't be intimidated into total silence. You have earned the right to be respected and earned the right to say what's on your mind and in your heart. You will always listen to what your kids tell you—in turn, they should always listen to you, even if they don't agree. Keep it short. Make your point, but don't go on and on.

4. Let the gospel predominate. God loves us *unconditionally*, and your adult children need to know that you unconditionally love them. What you're saying to them is only because you love them, not because you're trying to control them. It's not that you are trying to jam your life philosophy on them. You are just the messenger, passing on great news of great blessings.

5. If there are grandchildren in your family who are not being adequately cared for spiritually, then that means you know for sure what kinds of activities you're going to be doing when they're staying at your house. And without having to get all insulting about it to your daughter or to your son, when the grandkids are with you, that's when you teach them how to pray, that's when you bring them to church with you, that's when you bring out the God-talk, that's when you provide Bible story books on their level, that's when you just happen to have Bible story videos to watch.

6. Finally, pray like crazy. Your words to your spiritually struggling adult children may be *remembered*, even if not fully believed. Ultimately, the power to convert someone from lack of faith to faith has to come from God and his Word. It doesn't come from us. Do your best, and then let go and give it to God. And watch for new opportunities.

Bible Index

Old Testament

New Testament

Topical Index

more straight TALK

About the Writer

Pastor Mark Jeske brings the good news of Jesus Christ to viewers of *Time of Grace* in weekly 30-minute programs broadcast across America and around the world on local television, cable, and satellite, as well as on-demand streaming via the Internet. He is the senior pastor at St. Marcus Church, a thriving multicultural congregation in Milwaukee, Wisconsin. Mark is the author of several books and dozens of devotional booklets on various topics. He and his wife, Carol, have four adult children.

About Time of Grace

Time of Grace is for people who want more growth and less struggle in their spiritual walk. Through the timeless truth of God's Word, we connect people to God's grace so they know they are loved and forgiven and so they can start living in the freedom they've always wanted. To discover more, please visit timeofgrace.org or call 800.661.3311.

Help share God's message of grace!

Every gift you give helps Time of Grace reach people around the world with the good news of Jesus. Your generosity and prayer support take the gospel of grace to others through our ministry outreach and help them find the restart with Jesus they need.

Give today at timeofgrace.org/give or by calling 800.661.3311.

Thank you!